von Alfred Baur

# Grammar Tandem Activities

## Englisch, Klasse 7–10

Ernst Klett Verlag
Stuttgart · Leipzig

# Inhaltsverzeichnis


| | |
|---|---|
| Vorwort | 3 |
| Hinweise zu Fertigstellung und Einsatz des Arbeitsmaterials | 4 |
| Didaktisch-methodische Grundlagen | 5 |
| **1** Comparison of adjectives | 8 |
| **2a** Conditional sentences (type 1+2) | 13 |
| **2b** Conditional sentences (type 1–3) | 16 |
| **3** Relative clauses | 20 |
| **4** Asking questions | 26 |
| **5a** The passive | 30 |
| **5b** The passive | 36 |
| **5c** The passive | 41 |
| **6** Reported speech | 45 |
| **7** Grammar mix: Information for the teacher | 56 |
| **7** Grammar mix: Football for amateurs | 59 |
| **7** Grammar mix: Football for professionals | 62 |
| **7** Grammar mix: Tasks and results | 65 |
| **8** Mediation: Instructions | 75 |
| **8** Mediation: Situation 1: At the restaurant | 77 |
| **8** Mediation: Situation 2: At the hotel reception | 79 |
| **8** Mediation: Situation 3: Giving directions | 81 |
| **8** Mediation: Situation 4: On an exchange in a German family | 83 |
| Anhang: Aufkleber für Hängemappen | 85 |

## Liebe Kollegin, lieber Kollege,

„Grammar Tandem Activities" sind Übungsmaterialien für eigenverantwortliches Arbeiten von Schülerinnen und Schülern der Sekundarstufe und können in den Klassen 7–10 eingesetzt werden. Sie decken wichtige Grammatikthemen und Strukturen dieser Klassenstufen ab und schaffen durch wiederholtes Üben ein sicheres grammatisches Fundament, auf dem ein kreativer und lösungsoffener Sprachgebrauch aufbauen kann.
Hinter den „Grammar Tandem Activities" steht folgende Konzeption:

- Alle Übungen sind auf *mündlich-kommunikative Partnerarbeit* hin ausgerichtet. (Sie können jedoch auch als Kopiervorlagen für schriftliches Arbeiten benutzt werden.)
- Das *Material selbst steuert* die sprachlichen Äußerungen, so dass die *Ergebniskontrolle* über den Partner erfolgen kann. (*Partnercheck* als Selbstkontrolle)
- Alles Üben findet in einem *spielerischen Rahmen* statt, der das Zufallsprinzip mit einschließt und motivierend wirkt. Das Arbeitsmaterial bildet eine gelungene Synthese aus Arbeit und Spiel: *'Work and fun in one.'*

Die verschiedenen Themen werden jeweils durch *Instructions* eingeleitet. Diese sind alle gleich aufgebaut und liefern neben den notwendigen Sachinformationen auch die für eigenverantwortliches Arbeiten notwendige Orientierung. Die *Instructions*-Blätter sind folgendermaßen gegliedert:

- Oben erscheint das *Thema* mit einer *Checkliste* für das benötigte Spielzubehör in Form von *Bildsymbolen*. Es folgt eine Auflistung aller zum Arbeitsmaterial gehörigen Teile in Textform.
- 1. *Übungsgrundlage*: Sie gibt eine kurze *Erläuterung des grammatischen Problems*, die für eigenverantwortlich arbeitende Schülerinnen und Schüler verständlich ist, und enthält teilweise wertvolle *Lernhilfen*, z. B. in Form von Eselsbrücken.
- 2. *Übungsziel*: Hier wird – wie der Begriff schon sagt – kurz beschrieben, *was* eingeübt werden soll.
- 3. *Übungsweise*: Sie liefert eine *detaillierte Arbeitsanweisung* für den lerneffektiven Einsatz des Arbeitsmaterials, enthält die *Spielregeln* und beschreibt die Art der gegenseitigen *Ergebniskontrolle*.

Mit den „Grammar Tandem Activities" erwartet Sie und Ihre Klasse ein abwechslungsreiches und praxiserprobtes Übungsmaterial. Mit ihm können sogar Ihre Schülerinnen und Schüler der siebten bis zehnten Klassen ihre Grammatikkenntnisse „spielend" verbessern – und zwar ohne dass das von Ihnen vielleicht befürchtete Chaos ausbricht. Sie werden überrascht sein, wie gut das in der Praxis funktioniert, wenn Sie die Hinweise im nächsten Kapitel beachten.

Falls Sie neugierig geworden sind und den Versuch wagen wollen, wünsche ich Ihnen und Ihren Englischklassen viel Freude und Erfolg.

Alfred Bauer

## Hinweise zu Fertigstellung und Einsatz des Arbeitsmaterials

Durch *minimalen Arbeitsaufwand* können Sie die Kopiervorlagen zu den „Grammar Tandem Activities" in stabile Arbeitsmaterialien für eigenverantwortliches Arbeiten bzw. kommunikative Freiarbeit verwandeln, die durch viele Schülerhände gehen können, ohne Schaden zu nehmen.

Auf den Kopien selbst müssen Sie lediglich – wie auf den Kopiervorlagen angegeben – die betreffenden *Aufgabenblöcke in den Farben gelb, rot, blau und grün* hervorheben. Ob Sie das selbst tun oder von Ihren Schülerinnen und Schülern erledigen lassen, ob Sie dazu Holzfarbstifte, Textmarker oder entsprechend zugeschnittene Aufkleber verwenden, ist Ihnen überlassen.

Wichtig ist jedoch, dass Sie Ihre farbig markierten Kopien, die nur *einseitig* bedruckt sein dürfen, in *Folienhüllen* stecken und zwischen Vorder- und Rückseite mit einem auf DIN-A4 bzw. DIN-A5 *zugeschnittenen Pappkarton* (ca. 500 g/m²) verstärken. Wo Sie Pappkarton dieser Stärke günstig erwerben können, wissen mit Sicherheit Ihre Kolleginnen und Kollegen aus dem Fach Bildende Kunst. Große Formate sind erheblich billiger und lassen sich mit jeder Papierschneidemaschine auf die gewünschten DIN-Formate zuschneiden.

Wenn Sie alle zu einem bestimmten Grammatikthema gehörigen und mit Pappe verstärkten Kopien in ihren Folienhüllen in einer *Hängemappe* (Abb. 1) ablegen, die mit dem passenden *Aufkleber* aus dem *Anhang* des Kopiervorlagenhefts versehen ist, kann die Ausgabe und später die Rückgabe der Arbeitsmaterialien ohne Chaos sehr zügig und geordnet erfolgen. Ich empfehle Ihnen zu jedem der Grammatikthemen *mehrere Hängemappen* anzufertigen und diese in einem *Hängekorb* (Abb. 2) zu lagern, da dies die freie Themenwahl innerhalb der Klasse eher gewährleistet und Ihnen mehr pädagogischen Spielraum für die gezielte Wiederholung von einzelnen Grammatikthemen verschafft.

Nun fehlt nur noch das *Spielzubehör*. Wie auf den *Instructions* in Form von Bildsymbolen angegeben, benötigen Sie *Zahlenwürfel (1–6 Augen)* in zwei verschiedenen Farben, *Farbwürfel* mit den Farben *gelb, rot, blau, grün, schwarz und weiß*, sowie *Spielfiguren*, deren Farben Sie frei wählen können. Für das „Grammar mix"-Fußballspiel brauchen Sie zusätzlich eine Münze (1 Cent) als Ball. Das Spielzubehör können Sie bei *Lehrmittelverlagen* bestellen. Die Anzahl der benötigten Würfel und Spielfiguren kann mit Hilfe der Bildsymbole oben auf den *Instructions* leicht errechnet werden, hängt jedoch auch davon ab, wie viele Schülerpaare welches Grammatikthema zur gleichen Zeit bearbeiten können sollen.

Wenn Sie dieses Spielzubehör in ausreichender Zahl in einer *Box auf dem Lehrerpult* bereithalten und je nach Bedarf mit der entsprechenden Hängemappe ausgeben, wird Ihre Klasse innerhalb kürzester Zeit mit dem Arbeitsmaterial versorgt sein.

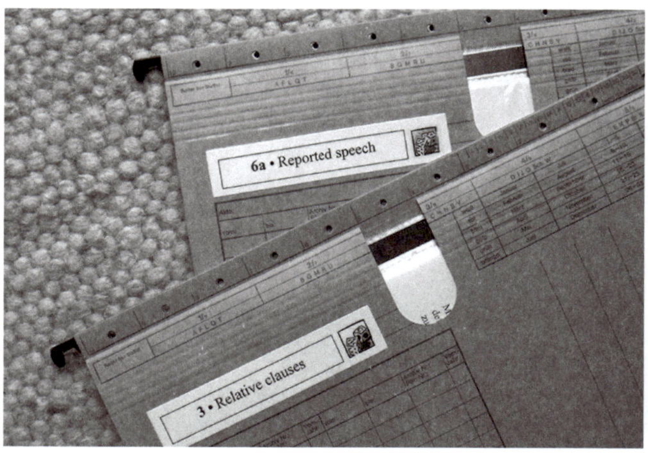

Abb. 1

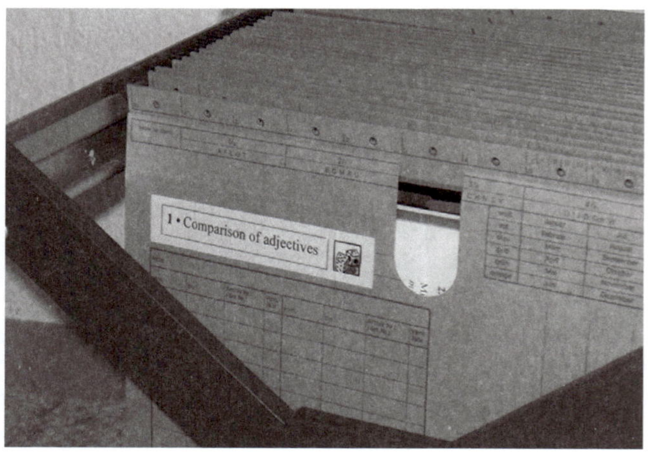

Abb. 2

# Didaktisch-methodische Grundlagen

Die Entwicklung der kommunikativen Kompetenz ist heute oberstes Ziel des Fremdsprachenunterrichts. Darunter versteht man die – durchaus mit Fehlern behaftete – allgemeine Fähigkeit zur sprachlichen Verständigung im Lebensalltag. Die Vermittlung *grammatischer Strukturen* ist diesem Ziel untergeordnet: Die Grammatik hat *dienende Funktion.*

### a) Lebendiges Arbeiten am „Skelett der Sprache"

Jeder Englischlehrer kennt zur Genüge sprachliche Äußerungen, bei denen man sehr wohl weiß, was gemeint ist, die aber fundamentale Regeln der englischen Sprache mit erstaunlicher Selbstverständlichkeit außer Acht lassen. Sie machen uns bewusst, dass Grammatik doch einen unverzichtbaren „Dienst" oder Beitrag zu echter Sprachkompetenz leistet, da sie der Sprache Form, Struktur und Ordnung gibt.

Was in der fachdidaktischen Literatur gerne als unbewusstes, allmähliches *Einschleifen* von grammatischen Strukturen bezeichnet wird, erweist sich im Unterrichtsalltag bei vielen Schülerinnen und Schülern als sehr mühsam und ist – um ehrlich zu sein – ohne bewusstes isoliertes Üben einer Struktur selten von Erfolg gekrönt. Das liegt daran, dass zum einen drei oder vier Unterrichtsstunden pro Woche dafür nicht ausreichen, und zum andern bei vielen Schülerinnen und Schülern kein ausgeprägtes *Sprachgefühl als Resonanzboden* vorhanden ist. Unter diesen Bedingungen wird Grammatikarbeit – um es bildhaft auszudrücken – schnell zu *harter Knochenarbeit am Skelett der Sprache.*

Das Vermitteln und Einüben grammatischer Strukturen und Regeln muss jedoch kein „totes Unterfangen" sein. Es kann sogar Spaß machen, wenn es methodisch interessant verpackt ist und auf *lebendige Weise* geschieht. In diesem Sinne versuchen die „Grammar Tandem Activities" die harte Knochenarbeit mit Freude am Lernen und Üben zu verbinden, indem Grammatikarbeit in einen spielerischen Rahmen eingebettet und in kommunikativer und kooperativer Form betrieben wird. So fühlt sich die Arbeit am Skelett der Sprache *lebendig* an.

### b) Nachhaltiges Lernen

Abb. 3

Tatsächlich bedarf es der *häufigen, bewussten Wiederholung* einer Struktur, damit diese sich nachhaltig einprägt. Erst dann hinterlässt Üben bei sehr vielen Schülerinnen und Schülern *feste Spuren im Langzeitgedächtnis* des Gehirns – gleich „Trampelpfaden" draußen in der Natur (Abb. 3), die Zeugnis davon ablegen, dass ein Weg schon oft gegangen worden ist. Der bei Pädagogen hochgeschätzte Hirnforscher und Neuro-Biologe Manfred Spitzer betont deshalb im Hinblick auf schulisches Lernen,

„ … dass es nicht darum gehen kann, stumpfsinnig Regeln auswendig zu lernen. Was Kinder brauchen, sind Beispiele. Sehr viele Beispiele und wenn möglich die richtigen und gute Beispiele. Auf die Regeln kommen sie dann schon selbst."[1)]

Deshalb enthalten die „Grammar Tandem Activities" insgesamt *500 Übungsbeispiele* und sind zudem auf *zyklisches Wiederholen* der jeweiligen grammatischen Strukturen hin konzipiert. Der spielerische Rahmen kann rein kooperativ oder mit Wettspielcharakter genutzt werden und beugt einer schnellen Ermüdung des Lernwillens vor. Gleichzeitig garantiert Partnerarbeit in kommunikativer Form durch viele Übungsbeispiele in kurzer Zeit ein *sehr hohes Maß an sprachlicher Umwälzung.* Der *Partnercheck* als Form der Selbstkontrolle durch den Lernpartner mit Hilfe des Arbeitsmaterials verhindert, dass sich falsche Sprachmuster einschleifen und vermittelt allmählich ein „Gefühl für sprachlich korrekte Lösungen".

[1)] Manfred Spitzer: Lernen: *Gehirnforschung und die Schule des Lebens;* Heidelberg, Berlin: Spektrum, Akademischer Verlag 2002, S. 78

Schließlich bieten die gut verständlichen *Instructions* die Möglichkeit, dass man sich vor oder während dem Üben die betreffenden Grammatikregeln auch nochmals *kognitiv* bewusst macht. So erfüllen die „Grammar Tandem Activities" alle Voraussetzungen für *nachhaltiges Lernen – mit Kopf, Herz und Hand.*

**c) Materialzentrierte kooperative Grammatikarbeit**

Der lehrerzentrierte Frontalunterricht wird heute gerade auch beim Fremdsprachenerwerb als veraltet und ineffektiv abgelehnt. Dabei hat er bei der Einführung und Bewusstmachung neuer grammatischer Strukturen mit Sicherheit seinen Platz. Beim (wiederholenden) Üben sind aber andere Übungs- und Sozialformen erfolgreicher.

Die „Grammar Tandem Activities" versuchen möglichst *alle* Schülerinnen und Schüler ihren *unterschiedlichen Begabungen gemäß* optimal zu fördern. Dazu stellen sie ein *differenziertes Angebot* an Übungen bereit. Reihenfolge, Arbeitstempo und die verwendete Übungszeit sind bei der Erledigung der Aufgaben individuell verschieden und den Fähigkeiten und speziellen Defiziten der Person angepasst.

Innere Differenzierung erfolgt also auf der Grundlage des Arbeitsmaterials, denn *optimale Förderung* lässt sich in leistungsheterogenen Gruppen nicht durch „lehrerzentriertes Lernen im Gleichschritt" realisieren. Sie erfordert eine Öffnung des Systems nach oben, so dass Leistungsspitzen ungehindert bis an ihre Grenzen über Mindeststandards hinauswachsen können.

Mit den „Grammar Tandem Activities" gehen Sie einen kleinen Schritt in Richtung *Individualisierung des Lernens*. Dabei sind (endlich einmal?) nicht Sie Dreh- und Angelpunkt des Unterrichtsgeschehens, sondern das Arbeitsmaterial. Ihre Person tritt zugunsten einer *materialzentrierten kooperativen Arbeitsweise* mit gegenseitiger Ergebniskontrolle durch die beiden Übungspartner in den Hintergrund. Sie als Lehrerin bzw. Lehrer werden für den Lernprozess „entbehrlich" – und damit frei für die individuelle Beratung und Förderung einzelner Schülerinnen und Schüler.

**d) Soziales Differenzieren**

Um alle Schülerinnen und Schüler mit ihren unterschiedlichen Begabungen optimal fördern zu können, bedarf es also eines differenzierten Lernangebots. Geschieht diese Individualisierung des Lernens jedoch in *Einzelkämpfermanier*, so dass es hauptsächlich darum geht andere zu übertrumpfen und auszustechen, dann bildet sich individuelle Fachkompetenz *auf Kosten von sozialer und personaler Kompetenz*. Der pädagogische Nutzen ist dabei fragwürdig. Das lässt sich vermeiden, wenn der Individualisierungsprozess des Lernens *sozial eingebunden* wird. Bei den „Grammar Tandem Activities" gelingt dies dadurch, dass *fachlich-inhaltliche Differenzierung* mit einer *sozial-kooperativen Arbeitsweise* verbunden ist. So betrachtet, könnte man diese Art des individualisierten Lernens als *soziales Differenzieren* bezeichnen.

Welche Gewichtung der soziale Aspekt dabei hat, hängt davon ab, wie Sie die Partnerarbeit organisieren. Die mögliche Bandbreite reicht von der *freien Wahl des Übungspartners* bis zu einem nach pädagogischen und sozialen Gesichtspunkten aufgebauten *Helfersystem*, innerhalb dessen die Lernenden ein hohes Maß an *Verantwortung* für sich selbst und füreinander in den Lernprozess einbringen.

### e) Eigenverantwortung und Motivation

Insgesamt wird deutlich, dass die „Grammar Tandem Activities" fachliche und personale Kompetenzen miteinander verknüpfen und so beide entwickeln helfen. Die spürbare *Eigenverantwortung* für den Lernfortschritt, die aus der schülerzentrierten, kooperativen Arbeitsform, der freien Wahl des Themas aus einer Reihe von Möglichkeiten und der spielerischen Art des Lernens hervorgeht, weckt bei vielen Schülerinnen und Schülern die sonst oft vermisste *intrinsische Motivation* und sorgt für eine lebendige und produktive Arbeitsatmosphäre.

Wenn Sie dieses Arbeitsmaterial zur zyklischen Wiederholung von Grammatik in für Sie und für Ihre Klassen angemessenen Zeitabständen einsetzen, wird von ihm sowohl in fachlicher als auch in sozialer Hinsicht eine positive Wirkung auf Ihre Englischklassen ausgehen. Der Reiz einer *etwas anderen Arbeitsform* wird für Ihre Schülerinnen und Schüler der Sekundarstufe eine willkommene Abwechslung sein, die Ihnen keine zusätzliche Arbeit macht, sondern Sie im Gegenteil spürbar entlastet durch eine *sich addierende Zeiteinsparung* bei der Unterrichtsvorbereitung.

**Anmerkung:**

Es folgen nun die Kopiervorlagen zu den verschiedenen Grammatikthemen. Lesen Sie stets aufmerksam die *Instructions*, bevor Sie die Arbeitsmaterialien fertigstellen. Achten Sie darauf, dass Sie fast durchweg *Partner A als Rückseite die Lösungen von Partner B* in die Folienhülle stecken *und umgekehrt*. Nur so ist die gegenseitige Ergebniskontrolle möglich.

Im Kopiervorlagenheft selbst orientiert sich die *Aufeinanderfolge der Kopiervorlagen* an diesem Schema. Wenn nun dennoch die „Aufgaben von Partner A" und die „Lösungen von Partner B" *nicht immer als Vorder- und Rückseite* sondern *teilweise nebeneinander* abgedruckt sind, so hängt das mit der Seitenzahl einzelner vorangehender Teilkapitel zusammen und erfordert von Ihnen beim Kopieren und Zusammenstellen der Arbeitsmaterialien erhöhte Aufmerksamkeit.

# 1 Comparison of adjectives

## Instructions

### Zum Arbeitsmaterial gehören:

1 Übungsanleitung *Instructions*, 1 Aufgabenblatt *Comparison of adjectives* für Partner A und Partner B, je 1 Lösungsblatt *Partner A: results* und *Partner B: results*, 1 Farbwürfel (gelb, rot, blau, grün, weiß, schwarz), 1 Würfel (1–6 Augen)

### 1. Übungsgrundlage:

Anders als im Deutschen gibt es im Englischen *zwei Arten der Steigerung* von Adjektiven. Welche Art der Steigerung angewandt werden muss, hängt von der *Zahl der Silben* ab, die das betreffende Adjektiv hat. Fast ohne Ausnahmen gilt:

*Einsilbige* Adjektive und *zweisilbige mit y-Endung* werden gesteigert, indem man *-er* bzw. *-est* anhängt. *Andere zweisilbige* und Adjektive mit *drei und mehr Silben* werden gesteigert, indem man *more* bzw. *most* voranstellt. Einige Adjektive, z. B. *good, bad, little* (= wenig), steigert man *unregelmäßig*. *Gleichheit* wird in einem Satz immer mit *as … as* wiedergegeben. *Ungleichheit* kann jedoch als *verneinte Gleichheit* (z. B. *not as ugly as*) oder durch die *1. Steigerungsform + than* (z. B. *nicer than / more beautiful than*) ausgedrückt werden.

### 2. Übungsziel:

Mit dem Arbeitmaterial soll geübt werden, Sachverhalte anhand von *Adjektiven mit unterschiedlicher Silbenzahl und Endung* in einem Satz zu vergleichen.

### 3. Übungsweise:

Beide Partner erhalten jeweils ein Aufgabenblatt mit jeweils 6 Vergleichen aus 6 verschiedenen Bereichen. Wie die Vergleiche ausfallen, ist durch *Symbole* (z. B. ▶ oder ▷ ) und in *Klammern stehende Adjektive* vorgegeben. Die Spieler würfeln *abwechselnd eine Farb-Zahl-Kombination* (z. B. blau 1) und bilden den fälligen Vergleich. Dabei gilt:

- Der Vergleich *zweier* Sachverhalte fällt immer zugunsten des Begriffs aus, auf den die *dunkle Pfeilspitze* ▶ zeigt. Mit diesem Begriff *beginnt* auch der Vergleichssatz.
- Bei *drei* zu vergleichenden Begriffen zeigt die dunkle Pfeilspitze auf den *größten / kleinsten / interessantesten* … Sachverhalt.
- Weitere Symbole: ◁=▷ (so … wie) ◀≠▷ (nicht so … wie)
- Beide Partner *korrigieren sich gegenseitig*. (Auf jedem Aufgabenblatt sind die Lösungen des Partners auf der Rückseite aufgelistet.)

Soll die Übung Wettspielcharakter haben, so erhält jeder Partner pro richtigen Vergleich *einen Punkt / Strich*, der auf einem Extrablatt notiert wird. Wer am Übungsende die meisten Punkte / Striche gesammelt hat, ist Sieger.


Grammar Tandem Activities
ISBN: 978-3-12-581180-5

# 1 Comparison of adjectives: Partner A

## free time (yellow)

1. staying at home ▶ going out (interesting)
2. being alone ◀≠▷ meeting friends (not funny)
3. ▷ listening to music ▶ making music ▷ going to a concert (creative / activity)
4. writing a text ◀ writing a letter (easy)
5. having hobbies ◀ hanging around (good)
6. watching a horror film ◀≠▷ watching a soap (not frightening)

## animals (green)

1. lions ◁=▷ tigers (dangerous)
2. animals in the wild ◀ animals in a zoo (feel / happy)
3. whales ▶ sharks (look / aggressive)
4. parrots ◁≠▶ chickens (not intelligent)
5. ▷ giraffes ▷ elephants ▶ mice (small / animals)
6. dogs ▶ cows (stupid)

## school (blue)

1. schooldays ◀ holidays (stressful)
2. young teachers ◀≠▷ old teachers (not experienced)
3. morning lessons ▶ afternoon lessons (hard)
4. ▷ the Maths book ▷ the English book ▶ the atlas (heavy / book)
5. ▷ an angry teacher ▶ a bad mark ▷ a boring lesson (bad / thing)
6. homework ◁=▷ tidying up your room (boring)

## travelling (red)

1. holidays in Turkey ◀ holidays in America (cheap)
2. sightseeing ▶ hiking (relaxing)
3. ▷ going by ship ▷ going by train ▶ going by plane (fast / way to travel)
4. ▷ Europe ▶ Asia ▷ Australia (large / continent on earth)
5. stony beaches ◀≠▷ sandy beaches (not popular)
6. snow-covered mountains ◁=▷ lonely islands (look / fascinating)

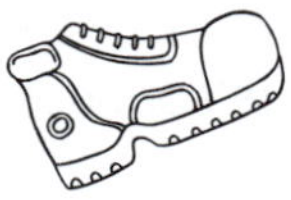

## lifestyle (black)

1. too much alcohol ◁=▷ smoking cigarettes (unhealthy)
2. ▶ doing sport ▷ watching sport on TV ▷ talking about sport (healthy / thing)
3. laptops ▶ mobile phones (expensive)
4. ▶ parties ▷ barbecues ▷ picnics (exciting / events)
5. friends ◀ success (important)
6. serious health problems ◀ financial problems (bad)

## environment (white)

1. Greenpeace ◁≠▶ Friends of the Earth (not famous)
2. ▶ riding a bike ▷ riding a motorbike ▷ going by bus (keep people / fit)
3. solar power ◀ nuclear power (safe)
4. public transport ▶ private transport (little / environmentally friendly)
5. driving alone ▶ sharing a car to work (good)
6. low pollution cars ◁=▷ low energy houses (useful)

Grammar Tandem Activities
ISBN: 978-3-12-581180-5

# 1 Comparison of adjectives: Partner B (results)

**sport:**

(yellow)

1. In the USA basketball is *more popular than* soccer.
2. Rugby players are *heavier than* racing drivers.
3. Golf is the sport of *the richest* people.
4. Football boots are *cheaper than* ski boots.
5. Ice skating is *as difficult as* in-line skating.
6. Bungee jumping is *the most dangerous* sport.

**food:**

(green)

1. Fresh fruit tastes *better than* fruit in tins.
2. Brown bread is *healthier than* white bread.
3. Hotels are *the most expensive* place.
4. Fatty food is *worse* for your health *than* fresh vegetables.
5. Lemonade is *the sweetest* drink.
6. Meat is *not as cheap as* eggs.

**England:**

(blue)

1. London is *the biggest* city.
2. French sounds *nicer than* English.
3. In the 19th century America was *not as powerful as* England.
4. English weather is *wetter than* German weather.
5. Fish and chips is *the most popular* fast food in Britain.
6. The North of England is *poorer than* the South of England.

**media:**

(red)

1. Written letters are *slower than* e-mails.
2. Telephones are *not as small as* mobile phones.
3. The documentary film seems *more interesting than* the talk show.
4. Classical music is *the oldest* style of music.
5. The Internet is *the most modern* medium.
6. Books are *more entertaining than* newspapers.

**jobs:**

(black)

1. Enjoying your job is *more important than* high wages.
2. Being out of work is *the worst* situation.
3. Factory work is *not as clean as* office work.
4. Nurses earn *less than* doctors.
5. Working alone is *more difficult than* teamwork.
6. Housewives work *as hard as* other workers.

**fashion:**

(white)

1. Designer clothes are *more expensive than* no-name products.
2. Working as a model is *as interesting as* designing clothes.
3. High-heeled shoes are *not as comfortable as* trainers.
4. The anorak seems *warmer than* the jacket.
5. School uniforms *don't* look *as fashionable as* trendy clothes.
6. Character is *the most important* thing.


Grammar Tandem Activities
ISBN: 978-3-12-581180-5

# 1 Comparison of adjectives: Partner B

## sport (yellow)

1. in the USA: basketball ◀ soccer (popular)
2. rugby players ◀ racing drivers (heavy)
3. ▷ tennis ▶ golf ▷ hockey (sport of rich people)
4. ski boots ▶ football boots (cheap)
5. ice skating ◁=▷ in-line skating (difficult)
6. ▷ skiing ▷ climbing ▶ bungee jumping (dangerous / sport)

## food (green)

1. fresh fruit ◀ fruit in tins (taste / good)
2. white bread ▶ brown bread (healthy)
3. ▷ restaurants ▷ snack bars ▶ hotels (expensive / place)
4. fresh vegetables ▶ fatty food (bad / for your health)
5. ▷ mineral water ▶ lemonade ▷ milk (sweet / drink)
6. meat ◀≠▷ eggs (not cheap)

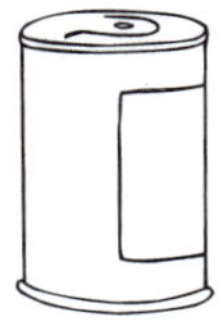

## England (blue)

1. ▶ London ▷ Manchester ▷ Dover (big / city)
2. French ◀ English (sound / nice)
3. 19th century: America ◀≠▷ England (not powerful)
4. English weather ◀ German weather (wet)
5. ▷ hamburgers ▶ fish and chips ▷ pizza (popular / fast food in Britain)
6. the South of England ▶ the North of England (poor)

## media (red)

1. written letters ◀ e-mails (slow)
2. telephones ◀≠▷ mobile phones (not small)
3. the documentary film ◀ the talk show (seem / interesting)
4. ▷ rock music ▷ hip-hop ▶ classical music (old / style of music)
5. ▷ television ▶ the Internet ▷ radio (modern / medium)
6. books ◀ newspapers (entertaining)

## jobs (black)

1. enjoying your job ◀ high wages (important)
2. ▷ working part-time ▶ being out of work ▷ being under stress (bad / situation)
3. factory work ◀≠▷ office work (not clean)
4. doctors ▶ nurses (earn / little)
5. teamwork ▶ working alone (difficult)
6. housewives ◁=▷ other workers (work / hard)

## fashion (white)

1. designer clothes ◀ no-name products (expensive)
2. working as a model ◁=▷ designing clothes (interesting)
3. high-heeled shoes ◀≠▷ trainers (not comfortable)
4. the anorak ◀ the jacket (seem / warm)
5. trendy clothes ◁≠▶ school uniforms (look / not fashionable)
6. ▷ clothing ▷ hairstyle ▶ character (important / thing)

Grammar Tandem Activities
ISBN: 978-3-12-581180-5

# 1 Comparison of adjectives: Partner A (results)

**free time:**

(yellow)

1. Going out is *more interesting than* staying at home.
2. Being alone is *not as funny as* meeting friends.
3. Making music is *the most creative* activity.
4. Writing a text is *easier than* writing a letter.
5. Having hobbies is *better than* hanging around.
6. Watching a soap is *not as frightening as* watching a horror film.

**animals:**

(green)

1. Lions are *as dangerous as* tigers.
2. Animals in the wild feel *happier than* animals in the zoo.
3. Sharks look *more aggressive than* whales.
4. Chickens are *not as intelligent as* parrots.
5. Mice are *the smallest* animals.
6. Cows are *more stupid than* dogs.

**school:**

(blue)

1. Schooldays are *more stressful than* holidays.
2. Young teachers are *not as experienced as* old teachers.
3. Afternoon lessons are *harder than* morning lessons.
4. The atlas is *the heaviest* book.
5. A bad mark is *the worst* thing.
6. Homework is *as boring as* tidying up your room.

**travelling:**

(red)

1. Holidays in Turkey *are cheaper than* holidays in America.
2. Hiking is *more relaxing than* sightseeing.
3. Going by plane is *the fastest* way to travel.
4. Asia is *the largest* continent on earth.
5. Stony beaches are *not as popular as* sandy beaches.
6. Snow-covered mountains look *as fascinating as* lonely islands.

**lifestyle:**

(black)

1. Too much alcohol is *as unhealthy as* smoking cigarettes.
2. Doing sport is *the healthiest* thing.
3. Laptops are *more expensive than* mobile phones.
4. Parties are *the most exciting* events.
5. Friends are *more important than* success.
6. Serious health problems are *worse than* financial problems.

**environment:**

(white)

1. Friends of the Earth are *not as famous as* Greenpeace.
2. Riding a bike keeps people *(the) fittest*.
3. Solar power is *safer than* nuclear power.
4. Private transport is *less* environmentally friendly *than* public transport.
5. Sharing a car to work is *better than* driving alone.
6 Low pollution cars are *as useful as* low energy houses.


Grammar Tandem Activities
ISBN: 978-3-12-581180-5

# 2a Conditional sentences (type 1+2)

## Instructions

### Zum Arbeitsmaterial gehören:

1 Übungsanleitung *Instructions*, 1 Spielfeld *Conditional sentences*, je 1 Aufgabenblatt *Conditional sentences (type 1+2)* für Partner A und Partner B, 1 Spielfigur, 1 Würfel (1–6 Augen)

### 1. Übungsgrundlage:

*Conditional sentences* sind Satzgefüge aus einem *If-Satz* und einem *Hauptsatz*. Der *If-Satz* nennt die Bedingung, der *Hauptsatz* die Folge. Die Zeiten im *If-Satz* und *Hauptsatz* bedingen sich gegenseitig, d.h. ist die Zeit in einem der beiden Satzteile bekannt, so ergibt sich daraus automatisch die Zeit im anderen Satzteil.
Man unterscheidet insgesamt drei verschiedene Typen von *Conditional sentences*.

### 2. Übungsziel:

Das Arbeitsmaterial dient dazu, die im *If-Satz* und *Hauptsatz* einander zugeordneten Zeiten bei den ersten zwei Typen von *Conditional sentences* einzuüben.

### 3. Übungsweise:

Beide Partner benutzen dasselbe Spielfeld und auch dieselbe Spielfigur. Sie beginnen bei *Start* und folgen dem Begriff *if*, indem sie jeweils um die gewürfelte Augenzahl vorrücken. Ab der zweiten Runde (es können beliebig viele gespielt werden) wird das Feld *Start* einfach ausgelassen.
Den Zahlen von 1–30, die auf dem Spielfeld doppelt vorkommen, ist jeweils *ein Conditional sentence* zugeordnet, der von beiden Partnern gemeinsam bearbeitet wird. Sie bilden die Zeiten in jenem *Conditional sentence*, auf dessen Zahl die Spielfigur gerade steht. Dabei gilt:

- Es beginnt stets derjenige Spieler, auf dessen Aufgabenblatt die *linke Satzhälfte normal gedruckt* ist und eine Lücke aufweist.
- Jeder Partner bildet nur *seine Hälfte* des Conditional sentence.
- Beide Partner *korrigieren sich gegenseitig*. (Auf jedem Aufgabenblatt ist die Lösung für die Satzhälfte des Partners *kursiv gedruckt*.)
- Auf *Deutsch* angegebene *Conditional sentences* werden *ganz* ins Englische übersetzt und vom Partner korrigiert.

Soll die Übung Wettspielcharakter haben, so erhält jeder Partner pro richtig eingesetzte Zeit *einen Punkt / Strich*, der auf einem Extrablatt notiert wird. Für fehlerfrei übersetzte *ganze Conditional sentences* gibt es jeweils *drei Punkte / Striche*. Wer am Übungsende die meisten Punkte / Striche gesammelt hat, ist Sieger.


ISBN: 978-3-12-581180-5

## 2 a Conditional sentences (type 1 + 2): Partner A

| | |
|---|---|
| 1. If we … , (walk) | *it would* take hours to get there.* |
| 2. *Stella will find the answer* | if she … carefully. (think) |
| 3. *If you lock your bike,* | thieves … it. (not steal) |
| 4. Girls … after him (not run) | *if he wasn't so famous.* |
| 5. *If we ask them for help,* | they … "no". (not say) |
| 6. If kids … so noisy and nervous, (not be) | *teaching them would* be more fun.* |
| 7. Ice hockey players … each other (hurt) | *if they didn't wear helmets.* |
| 8. *Jim and David won't play outside* | if it … all the time. (rain) |
| 9. *If the kids had a mobile with them,* | we … them now. (phone) |
| 10. If I … hungry, (not be) | *I won't eat anything for lunch.* |
| 11. *Carol wouldn't look so pretty* | if she … her hair short. (cut) |
| 12. *If you are tired,* | we … a short break. (take) |
| 13. Mr Hill … always … his job (not lose) | *if he worked harder.* |
| 14. *If Jonah doesn't go to bed now,* | he … tired at school tomorrow. (feel) |
| 15. If she … at home, (not be) | *I will send her a text message.* |
| 16. If children … sport, (not do) | *they wouldn't* have so much fun.* |
| 17. *If somebody doesn't like guitars,* | he / she … music by 'The Beatles'. (not like) |
| 18. Liz … very sad (feel) | *if Terry didn't remember her birthday.* |
| 19. If Jim … his teeth after meals, (clean) | *he won't get trouble with them.* |
| 20. *If there were more exercises like that,* | most students … grammar lessons. (enjoy) |
| 21. If Tilly … her room, (not tidy) | *her mum would tell her to do it.* |
| 22. *Max will choose the bike as a prize* | if he … the winning number. (have) |

23. *If Jack packs his school bag in the evening, he won't forget so many things.*

24. Wenn Sophie laute Musik hören würde, würde sie das Telefon nicht hören.

25. *We wouldn't find our way if we didn't use a map.*

26. Die Gäste würden nicht singen und tanzen, wenn die Party langweilig wäre.

27. *I will phone you if my train is late.*

28. Niemand wird dich verstehen, wenn du nicht laut genug sprichst.

29. *If our guests got up now, we could have / eat breakfast together.*

30. Wenn ich (es) nicht vergesse, werde ich dir ein Souvenir kaufen.

* In these sentences *would / could / might* and *wouldn't / couldn't / mightn't* can replace each other.


Grammar Tandem Activities
ISBN: 978-3-12-581180-5

## 2a Conditional sentences (type 1+2): Partner B

| | |
|---|---|
| 1. *If we walked,* | it … hours to get there. (take) |
| 2. Stella … the answer (find) | *if she thinks carefully.* |
| 3. If you … your bike, (lock) | *thieves won't steal it.* |
| 4. *Girls wouldn't run after him* | if he … so famous. (not be) |
| 5. If we … them for help, (ask) | *they won't say "no".* |
| 6. *If kids weren't so noisy and nervous,* | teaching them … more fun. (be) |
| 7. *Ice hockey players would* hurt each other* | if they … helmets. (not wear) |
| 8. Jim and David … outside, (not play) | *if it rains all the time.* |
| 9. If the kids … a mobile with them, (have) | *we could* phone them now.* |
| 10. *If I'm not hungry,* | I … anything for lunch. (not eat) |
| 11. Carol … so pretty (not look) | *if she cut her hair short.* |
| 12. If you … tired, (be) | *we will take a short break.* |
| 13. *Mr Hill wouldn't always lose his job* | if he … harder. (work) |
| 14. If Jonah … to bed now, (not go) | *he will feel tired at school tomorrow.* |
| 15. *If she isn't at home,* | I … her a text message. (send) |
| 16. *If children didn't do sport,* | they … so much fun. (not have) |
| 17. If somebody … guitars, (not like) | *he/she won't like music by 'The Beatles'.* |
| 18. *Liz would feel very sad* | if Terry … her birthday. (not remember) |
| 19. *If Jim cleans his teeth after meals,* | he … trouble with them. (not get) |
| 20. If there … more exercises like that, (be) | *most students would* enjoy grammar lessons.* |
| 21. *If Tilly didn't tidy her room,* | her mum … her to do it. (tell) |
| 22. Max … the bike as a prize (choose) | *if he has the winning number.* |

23. Wenn Jack seine Schultasche am Abend packt, wird er nicht so viele Dinge vergessen.
24. *If Sophie listened to loud music, she wouldn't hear the telephone.*
25. Wir würden unsern Weg nicht finden, wenn wir nicht eine Landkarte benutzen würden.
26. *The guests wouldn't sing and dance if the party was boring.*
27. Ich werde dich anrufen, wenn mein Zug Verspätung hat.
28. *Nobody will understand you if you don't speak loud enough.*
29. Wenn unsere Gäste jetzt aufstehen würden, könnten wir zusammen frühstücken.
30. *If I don't forget, I will buy you a souvenir.*

* In these sentences *would/could/might* and *wouldn't/couldn't/mightn't* can replace each other.

Grammar Tandem Activities
ISBN: 978-3-12-581180-5

# 2b Conditional sentences (type 1–3)

## Instructions

### Zum Arbeitsmaterial gehören:

1 Übungsanleitung *Instructions*, 1 Spielfeld *Conditional sentences*, je 1 Aufgabenblatt *Conditional sentences (type 1–3)* für Partner A und Partner B, 1 Spielfigur, 1 Würfel (1–6 Augen)

### 1. Übungsgrundlage:

*Conditional sentences* sind Satzgefüge aus einem *If-Satz* und einem *Hauptsatz*. Der *If-Satz* nennt die Bedingung, der *Hauptsatz* die Folge. Die Zeiten im *If-Satz* und *Hauptsatz* bedingen sich gegenseitig, d.h. ist die Zeit in einem der beiden Satzteile bekannt, so ergibt sich daraus automatisch die Zeit im anderen Satzteil.
Man unterscheidet insgesamt drei verschiedene Typen von *Conditional sentences*.

### 2. Übungsziel:

Das Arbeitsmaterial dient dazu, die im *If-Satz* und *Hauptsatz* einander zugeordneten Zeiten bei allen drei Typen von *Conditional sentences* einzuüben.

### 3. Übungsweise:

Beide Partner benutzen dasselbe Spielfeld und auch dieselbe Spielfigur. Sie beginnen bei *Start* und folgen dem Begriff *if*, indem sie jeweils um die gewürfelte Augenzahl vorrücken. Ab der zweiten Runde (es können beliebig viele gespielt werden) wird das Feld *Start* einfach ausgelassen.
Den Zahlen von 1–30, die auf dem Spielfeld doppelt vorkommen, ist jeweils *ein Conditional sentence* zugeordnet, der von beiden Partnern gemeinsam bearbeitet wird. Sie bilden die Zeiten in jenem *Conditional sentence*, auf dessen Zahl die Spielfigur gerade steht. Dabei gilt:

- Es beginnt stets derjenige Spieler, auf dessen Aufgabenblatt die *linke Satzhälfte normal gedruckt* ist und eine Lücke aufweist.
- Jeder Partner bildet nur *seine Hälfte* des Conditional sentence.
- Beide Partner *korrigieren sich gegenseitig*. (Auf jedem Aufgabenblatt ist die Lösung für die Satzhälfte des Partners *kursiv gedruckt*.)
- Auf *Deutsch* angegebene *Conditional sentences* werden *ganz* ins Englische übersetzt und vom Partner korrigiert.

Soll die Übung Wettspielcharakter haben, so erhält jeder Partner pro richtig eingesetzte Zeit *einen Punkt / Strich*, der auf einem Extrablatt notiert wird. Für fehlerfrei übersetzte *ganze Conditional sentences* gibt es jeweils *drei Punkte / Striche*. Wer am Übungsende die meisten Punkte / Striche gesammelt hat, ist Sieger.


ISBN: 978-3-12-581180-5

## 2b Conditional sentences (type 1–3): Partner A

| | |
|---|---|
| 1. *Alex will invite Susan for a drink* | if he … her at the disco. (meet) |
| 2. Our team … every match (not lose) | *if we practised more often.* |
| 3. *Grandfather would* have died* | if he … to hospital. (not go) |
| 4. *If Aunt Victoria travels to Paris,* | she … the Eiffel Tower. (visit) |
| 5. If I … you, (be) | *I would go and see a doctor, of course.* |
| 6. *Your teacher will talk to your parents* | if you … your homework. (not do) |
| 7. If we … our umbrellas, (take) | *we wouldn't* have got wet through.* |
| 8. *If the fridge doesn't work,* | the food … bad. (go) |
| 9. If Sarah … in the holidays, (not work) | *she couldn't pay for those expensive clothes.* |
| 10. You … your fingers (cut) | *if you aren't careful with that knife.* |
| 11. *Alan would* have taken a photo* | if he … a camera. (have) |
| 12. Anne … a lot of time (save) | *if she had gone by plane.* |
| 13. If you … museums, (not like) | *we won't visit any of them.* |
| 14. *If the weather didn't change,* | they … the weekend on the beach. (spend) |
| 15. *If Cathy had played well,* | she … that match. (win) |
| 16. *Little Tom could* ride his bike again* | if somebody … it. (repair) |
| 17. If I … at home again, (be) | *I will write you a letter.* |
| 18. It … our environment (help) | *if more people used public transport.* |
| 19. *If he had told me his troubles,* | I … to help him. (try) |
| 20. *Football wouldn't* be so popular* | if it … so exciting. (not be) |
| 21. *If you don't like this room,* | I … you another. (show) |
| 22. If Peter … so many mistakes, (not make) | *English would* be more fun for him.* |

23. Wenn Marvin sich beeilt hätte, hätte er den Schulbus nicht verpasst.
24. *If Laura had given a birthday party, she would have invited me.*
25. Wenn Papa jetzt nach Hause käme, könnten wir zu Mittag essen.
26. *If Gina doesn't come, Colin will go without her.*
27. Wenn das Baby nicht müde ist, wird es nicht schlafen.
28. *If I had the opportunity/chance, I would travel to Africa.*
29. Ich würde sie auf meinem Heimweg besuchen, wenn ich ihre Adresse wüsste.
30. *One day Joe will have an accident if he drives too fast.*

* In these sentences *would/could/might* and *wouldn't/couldn't/mightn't* can replace each other.

Grammar Tandem Activities
ISBN: 978-3-12-581180-5

## 2b Conditional sentences (type 1–3): Partner B

| | |
|---|---|
| 1. Alex … Susan for a drink (invite) | _if he meets her at the disco._ |
| 2. _Our team wouldn't* lose every match_ | if we … more often. (practise) |
| 3. Grandfather … (die) | _if he hadn't gone to hospital._ |
| 4. If Aunt Victoria … to Paris, (travel) | _she will visit the Eiffel Tower._ |
| 5. _If I were you,_ | I … a doctor, of course. (go and see) |
| 6. Your teacher … to your parents (talk) | _if you don't do your homework._ |
| 7. _If we had taken our umbrellas,_ | we … wet through. (not get) |
| 8. If the fridge … , (not work) | _the food will go bad._ |
| 9. _If Sarah didn't work in the holidays,_ | she … for those expensive clothes. (not pay) |
| 10. _You will cut your fingers_ | if you … careful with that knife. (not be) |
| 11. Alan … a photo (take) | _if he had had a camera._ |
| 12. _Anne would* have saved a lot of time_ | if she … by plane. (go) |
| 13. _If you don't like museums,_ | we … any of them. (not visit) |
| 14. If the weather … , (not change) | _they would* spend the weekend on the beach._ |
| 15. If Cathy … well, (play) | _she would* have won that match._ |
| 16. Little Tom … his bike again (ride) | _if somebody repaired it._ |
| 17. _If I am at home again,_ | I … you a letter. (write) |
| 18. _It would help our environment_ | if more people … public transport. (use) |
| 19. If he … me his troubles, (tell) | _I would* have tried to help him._ |
| 20. Football … so popular (not be) | _if it wasn't so exciting._ |
| 21. If you … this room, (not like) | _I will show you another._ |
| 22. _If Peter didn't make so many mistakes,_ | English … more fun for him. (be) |

23. _If Marvin had hurried, he wouldn't have missed the school bus._

24. Wenn Laura eine Geburtstagsparty gegeben hätte, hätte sie mich eingeladen.

25. _If Dad came home now, we could have / eat lunch._

26. Wenn Gina nicht kommt, wird Colin ohne sie gehen.

27. _If the baby isn't tired, it won't sleep._

28. Wenn ich die Möglichkeit / Chance hätte, würde ich nach Afrika reisen.

29. _I would visit her on my way home if I knew her address._

30. Eines Tages wird Joe einen Unfall haben, wenn er zu schnell fährt.

* In these sentences _would / could / might_ and _wouldn't / couldn't / mightn't_ can replace each other.


Grammar Tandem Activities
ISBN: 978-3-12-581180-5

## 2ab Conditional sentences: Spielfeld

ISBN: 978-3-12-581180-5

# 3 Relative clauses

## Instructions

### Zum Arbeitsmaterial gehören:

1 Übungsanleitung *Instructions*, 1 Blatt *Words to define*, je 1 *Mind map* für Partner A und Partner B, je 1 Lösungsblatt *Partner A: results* und *Partner B: results*, 1 Farbwürfel (gelb, rot, blau, grün, weiß, schwarz), 1 Würfel (1–6 Augen)

### 1. Übungsgrundlage:

Relativsätze werden durch ein *Relativpronomen (who, which, whose)* eingeleitet. Das Relativpronomen steht (fast immer) direkt *hinter dem Bezugswort*, auf das es sich bezieht. Dieses Bezugswort wird vom Relativsatz näher beschrieben oder definiert. Handelt es sich beim Bezugswort um *Personen*, so benutzt man *who*, handelt es sich um *Dinge oder Tiere*, so benutzt man *which*. (Da sich *that* als Relativpronomen auf Personen, Dinge *und* Tiere beziehen kann, stellt es kein Problem dar und darf deshalb hier nicht benutzt werden.)
Beachte bitte: Auch *whose* kann bei Personen, Dingen und Tieren benutzt werden, bedeutet jedoch *dessen / deren*.

### 2. Übungsziel:

Mit dem Arbeitsmaterial soll geübt werden, wie *Hauptwörter* durch Relativsätze definiert werden können, wobei nur *who / which / whose* als Relativpronomen zur Verfügung stehen.

### 3. Übungsweise:

Die beiden Partner erhalten jeder eine Sammlung von 3 x 6 Begriffen aus verschiedenen Bereichen (= ihre Blatthälfte *Words to define*) und die dazugehörige *Mind map*, welche die Oberbegriffe (z. B. *vehicles*) und inhaltliches Sprachmaterial für die einzelnen Definitionen enthält. Auf der Rückseite sind die Lösungen des Partners aufkopiert.
Die Spieler würfeln *abwechselnd eine Farb-Zahl-Kombination* (z. B. gelb 3). Wer die gewürfelte Farbe (und auch Zahl) auf seiner *Mind map* vorfindet, bildet die dazugehörige Definition.
Es empfiehlt sich folgendes Vorgehen:

- *Sprachmaterial* zur Farb-Zahl-Kombination aufmerksam lesen.
- Welcher Begriff aus der Sammlung *Words to define* passt dazu?
- Welches *Relativpronomen* ist hier korrekt?
- Definition als *Relativsatz* bilden und sich *gegenseitig korrigieren*.

Soll die Übung Wettspielcharakter haben, so erhält jeder Partner *einen Punkt / Strich* für das richtige Relativpronomen. Für eine vollkommen fehlerfreie Definition gibt es *zwei Punkte / Striche*. Diese werden auf einem Extrablatt notiert. Wer am Übungsende die meisten Punkte / Striche gesammelt hat, ist Sieger.


ISBN: 978-3-12-581180-5

## 3 Relative clauses: Words to define (Partner A)

(yellow)

underground trains
a ferry
an ambulance
caravans
a tractor
spaceships

(red)

pop stars
vegetarians
a housewife
a criminal
a model
mechanics

(white)

a skyscraper
castles
discos
a church
a museum of art
hotels

---

## 3 Relative clauses: Words to define (Partner B)

(green)

pigs
a parrot
a snake
horses
cats
an elephant

(blue)

a lift or elevator
a computer
vacuum cleaners
a mobile (phone)
a freezer
an alarm clock

(black)

glasses
a bicycle bell
a souvenir
a crash helmet
toys
special offers

Grammar Tandem Activities
ISBN: 978-3-12-581180-5

# 3 Relative clauses: Mind map (Partner A)

**Relative clauses**
**with *who / which / whose***

(yellow)
**vehicle(s)**

1. back wheels / very big
2. go / system of tunnels / below ground
3. transport / cars, buses and passengers / the sea
4. people / live / while / on holiday
5. top speed / thousands of kilometres / hour
6. take / sick or injured people / hospital

(red)
**somebody / people**
**woman**

1. do the housework / look after / children
2. repair / vehicles / garage
3. beauty / used / sell products
4. not eat / meat
5. songs you can buy / CDs / or download / money
6. do things / be against the law

(white)
**building(s) / place(s)**

1. very tall / because / have lots of floors
2. tower / higher / the houses / neighbourhood
3. owners in the past / kings, queens or noblemen
4. rooms you can book / when / journey or holiday
5. young people / go / if / want to dance
6. invite / visitors / look at / famous works of art


Grammar Tandem Activities
ISBN: 978-3-12-581180-5

## 3 Relative clauses: Partner B (results)

(green)

1. Cats are pets / animals *which* can hurt you with their teeth and claws.
2. Pigs are animals *whose* meat is used to make sausages and steaks.
3. An elephant is an animal *whose* skin is grey and *(whose)* weight can be several tons.
4. A parrot is an animal / a pet *which* is very colourful and *(which* is*)* good at saying words.
5. Horses are animals *which* live in stables and *(which)* people ride as a hobby.
6. A snake is an animal *which* moves very fast although it has no legs.

(blue)

1. A mobile (phone) is an electronic device[1] *which* you (can) phone, take photos and play games on.
2. A freezer is a machine *whose* inside temperature is so low that food doesn't go bad.
3. A lift or elevator is a machine *which* takes people and things up or down to another floor.
4. A computer is an electronic device[1] *which* connects offices and private Internet users to / with the worldwide web.
5. An alarm clock is an electronic device[1] *whose* sound wakes people up in the mornings.
6. Vacuum cleaners are machines *which* take up (the) dirt from floors and carpets.

(black)

1. A crash helmet is something *which* protects a rider's head in an accident.
2. Glasses are things *which* people wear on their nose if they have poor eyes.
3. A bicycle bell is something *whose* sound warns other cyclists or people
4. A souvenir is something *which* tourists buy that they don't forget their holiday.
5. Special offers are things *whose* price is very low at the moment.
6. Toys are things *which* children play with in their free time.

[1] electronic device = *elektronisches Gerät*


ISBN: 978-3-12-581180-5

# 3 Relative clauses: Mind map (Partner B)

**Relative clauses with *who / which / whose***

(green) **pet(s) / animal(s)**

1. can hurt you / teeth and claws
2. meat / used / make sausages and steaks
3. skin / grey / weight can be several tons
4. very colourful / good at / say words
5. live / stables / people / ride / hobby
6. move / very fast / although / have no legs

(blue) **machine(s)** / **electronic device**[1]

1. you / phone / take photos / play games
2. inside temperature / so low / food / not go bad
3. take / people and things / up or down / another floor
4. connect / offices / private Internet users / worldwide web
5. sound / wake people up / mornings
6. take up / dirt / floors and carpets

(black) **something / things**

1. protect / a rider's head / accident
2. people / wear / nose / if / have poor eyes
3. sound / warn / other cyclists or people
4. tourists / buy / that / not forget / their holiday
5. price / very low / at the moment
6. children / play / their free time

[1] electronic device = elektronisches Gerät


Grammar Tandem Activities
ISBN: 978-3-12-581180-5

# 3 Relative clauses: Partner A (results)

(yellow)

1. A tractor is a vehicle *whose* back wheels are very big.
2. Underground trains are vehicles *which* go through a system of tunnels below ground.
3. A ferry is a vehicle *which* transports cars, buses and passengers across / over the sea.
4. Caravans are vehicles *which* people live in while they are on holiday.
5. Spaceships are vehicles *whose* top speed is thousands of kilometres an / per hour.
6. An ambulance is a vehicle *which* takes sick or injured people to hospital.

(red)

1. A housewife is a woman *who* does the housework and looks after the children.
2. Mechanics are people *who* repair vehicles at a garage.
3. A model is somebody *whose* beauty is used to sell products.
4. Vegetarians are people *who* don't eat (any) meat.
5. Pop stars are people *whose* songs you can buy on CDs or download for money.
6. A criminal is somebody *who* does things *which* are against the law.

(white)

1. A skyscraper is a building *which* is very tall, because it has lots of floors.
2. A church is a building *whose* tower is higher than the houses in the neighbourhood.
3. Castles are buildings *whose* owners in the past were kings, queens or noblemen.
4. Hotels are buildings *whose* rooms you can book when you go on a journey or holiday.
5. Discos are places / buildings *which* young people go to if they want to dance.
6. A museum of art is a place / building *which* invites visitors to look at famous works of art.

Grammar Tandem Activities
ISBN: 978-3-12-581180-5

# 4 Asking questions

## Instructions

### Zum Arbeitsmaterial gehören:

1 Übungsanleitung *Instructions*, 1 Spielfeld *Asking questions*, je 1 Aufgabenblatt *Asking questions* für Partner A und Partner B mit den Lösungen (*results*) des Partners, 1 Spielfigur, 1 Würfel (1–6 Augen)

### 1. Übungsgrundlage:

Anders als im Deutschen wird für die Bildung von Fragen im Englischen fast immer ein *Hilfsverb* gebraucht. Ist keines vorhanden, so wird eines hinzugezogen, wie z. B. *do* bzw. *does* (beim *simple present*) oder *did* (beim *simple past*). Der folgende Reim und die beiden Bilder dazu machen diesen Sachverhalt anschaulich und gelten bis auf wenige Ausnahmen:

Liebe Schüler, lasst euch sagen,
auf ***zwei Beinen*** stehen Fragen!
Bei ***who*** (= wer) und ***be*** (= sein)
stehen sie jedoch auf ***einem*** Bein.

Beachte jedoch:
Fragen mit ***who*** = ***wem*** oder ***wen*** werden mit einem Hilfsverb gebildet.

### 2. Übungsziel:

Das Arbeitsmaterial dient dazu, die Bildung von Fragen (*simple present, simple past, present perfect, will-future, auxiliary + verb*) mit den Fragewörtern *what, when, where, why, which, who, how (long / many …)* einzuüben.

### 3. Übungsweise:

Beide Partner benutzen dasselbe Spielfeld und auch dieselbe Spielfigur. Sie beginnen bei *Start* und folgen dem *Fragezeichen*, indem sie stets um die gewürfelte Augenzahl vorrücken. Ab der zweiten Runde (es können beliebig viele gespielt werden) wird das Feld *Start* einfach ausgelassen.
Den Zahlen von 1–18, die auf dem Spielfeld doppelt vorkommen, ist auf jedem Aufgabenblatt jeweils *ein Satz* zugeordnet. Landet die Spielfigur zum Beispiel auf Feld 8, so bildet der Spieler, der soeben gewürfelt hat, die zu Satz 8 auf seinem Aufgabenblatt *passende Frage*. Dabei gilt:

- Die Frage muss so formuliert werden, dass der *im Satz unterstrichene* Begriff oder Satzteil die *Antwort* auf diese Frage darstellt.
- Schau dir das im Satz *kursiv gedruckte Verb* genau an, denn …
  … es muss auch in der Frage verwendet werden.
  … es zeigt dir, in welcher *Zeit* die Frage gestellt werden muss.
- Beide Partner *korrigieren sich gegenseitig*. (Unten auf jedem Aufgabenblatt sind die Lösungen des Partners aufgelistet.)

Soll die Übung Wettspielcharakter haben, so erhält jeder Partner pro richtig gebildete Frage *einen Punkt / Strich*, der auf einem Extrablatt notiert wird. Wer am Übungsende die meisten Punkte / Striche gesammelt hat, ist Sieger.


Grammar Tandem Activities
ISBN: 978-3-12-581180-5

## 4 Asking questions: Partner A

1. Sarah and Jane *work* as nurses at a hospital in Dublin.
2. He *fell* ill because he smoked thirty cigarettes a day.
3. Robert *has* already *done* his homework for next Monday.
4. Yesterday a good friend of mine *broke* his leg in a motorcycle accident.
5. A car ferry *can carry* hundreds of vehicles.
6. The concert *was* so fantastic because the band played all their greatest hits.
7. They *have known* each other since they were little children.
8. The guests from Spain *will arrive* next weekend.
9. Luke has got three teddy bears, but he *likes* his panda best.
10. Mr Wilkins often *phones* his wife and his children while he is on business trips.
11. The police *caught* the criminals in a nearby forest.
12. Aunt Agatha sometimes *talks to* herself in the mirror.
13. If possible Alan *does* his homework after lunch.
14. You *can get* more information on our home page.
15. There are several big cities in Europe, but London *is* the biggest of them.
16. Clare and her friends *got* home from the disco by taxi.
17. Carl Benz *developed* the first car with a petrol engine in the 1890s.
18. Mrs Wellington *has moved* to Philadelphia because her husband found a new job there.

---

## 4 Asking questions: Partner B (results)

1. When *did* Mum *lose* her wedding ring?
2. What *does* Eve usually *have* for breakfast?
3. Why *won't* Alex *pass* his exam?
4. Where *were* Marvin's football boots?
5. How much *is* the flight to Singapore?
6. Who *cooks* lunch for his family on Sundays?
7. What *did* the boys (only) *talk about*?
8. Where *do* Sue and her boyfriend Ray *meet*?
9. When *did* baby Alice *wake up*?
10. Why *did* two football hooligans *start* a fight?
11. Which T-shirt *did* Jacky *take*?
12. Where *did* the Shaws *spend* their holidays?
13. Why *does* Eve often *change* her hairstyle?
14. How *do* stars often *celebrate* their birthday?
15. Who *did* a store detective *watch* (putting CDs into their handbags)?
16. How long *did* his dangerous heart operation *take*?
17. When *do* Mr and Mrs Howard *get up* on workdays?
18. Who *became* the first black president of the United States in 2009?

Grammar Tandem Activities
ISBN: 978-3-12-581180-5

## 4 Asking questions: Partner B

1. Mum *lost* her wedding ring while she was working in the garden.
2. Eve usually *has* cornflakes for breakfast.
3. Alex *won't pass* his exam because he doesn't do anything for school.
4. Marvin's football boots *were* in Simon's sports bag.
5. The flight to Singapore *is* 949 euros.
6. On Sundays Uncle Raymond *cooks* lunch for his family.
7. Anna's party was boring because the boys only *talked about* football.
8. Sue and her boyfriend Ray *meet* in the park every afternoon.
9. Baby Alice *woke up* an hour ago.
10. Two football hooligans *started* a fight because their team had lost the match.
11. Jacky could choose from five beautiful T-shirts – and she *took* the pink one.
12. The Shaws *spent* their holidays somewhere on the coast.
13. Eve often *changes* her hairstyle because she wants to look attractive.
14. Stars often *celebrate* their birthday with an expensive party.
15. A store detective *watched* a group of girls putting CDs into their handbags.
16. His dangerous heart operation *took* more than six hours.
17. On workdays Mr and Mrs Howard *get up* at half past five.
18. In 2009 Barack Obama *became* the first black president of the United States.

---

## 4 Asking questions: Partner A (results)

1. Where *do* Sarah and Jane *work*?
2. Why *did* he *fall* ill?
3. What *has* Robert already *done*?
4. Who *broke* his leg in a motorcycle accident?
5. How many vehicles *can* a car ferry *carry*?
6. Why *was* the concert so fantastic?
7. How long *have* they *known* each other?
8. When *will* the guests from Spain *arrive*?
9. Which teddy bear / animal *does* Luke *like* best?
10. Who *does* Mr Wilkins often *phone*?
11. Where *did* the police *catch* the criminals?
12. Who *does* Aunt Agatha sometimes *talk to*?
13. When *does* Alan *do* his homework?
14. Where *can* you *get* more information?
15. Which *is* the biggest (city)? / Which *is* the biggest city in Europe?
16. How *did* Clare and her friends *get* home from the disco?
17. When *did* Carl Benz *develop* the first car with a petrol engine?
18. Why *has* Mrs Wellington *moved* to Philadelphia?


Grammar Tandem Activities
ISBN: 978-3-12-581180-5

## 4 Asking questions: Spielfeld

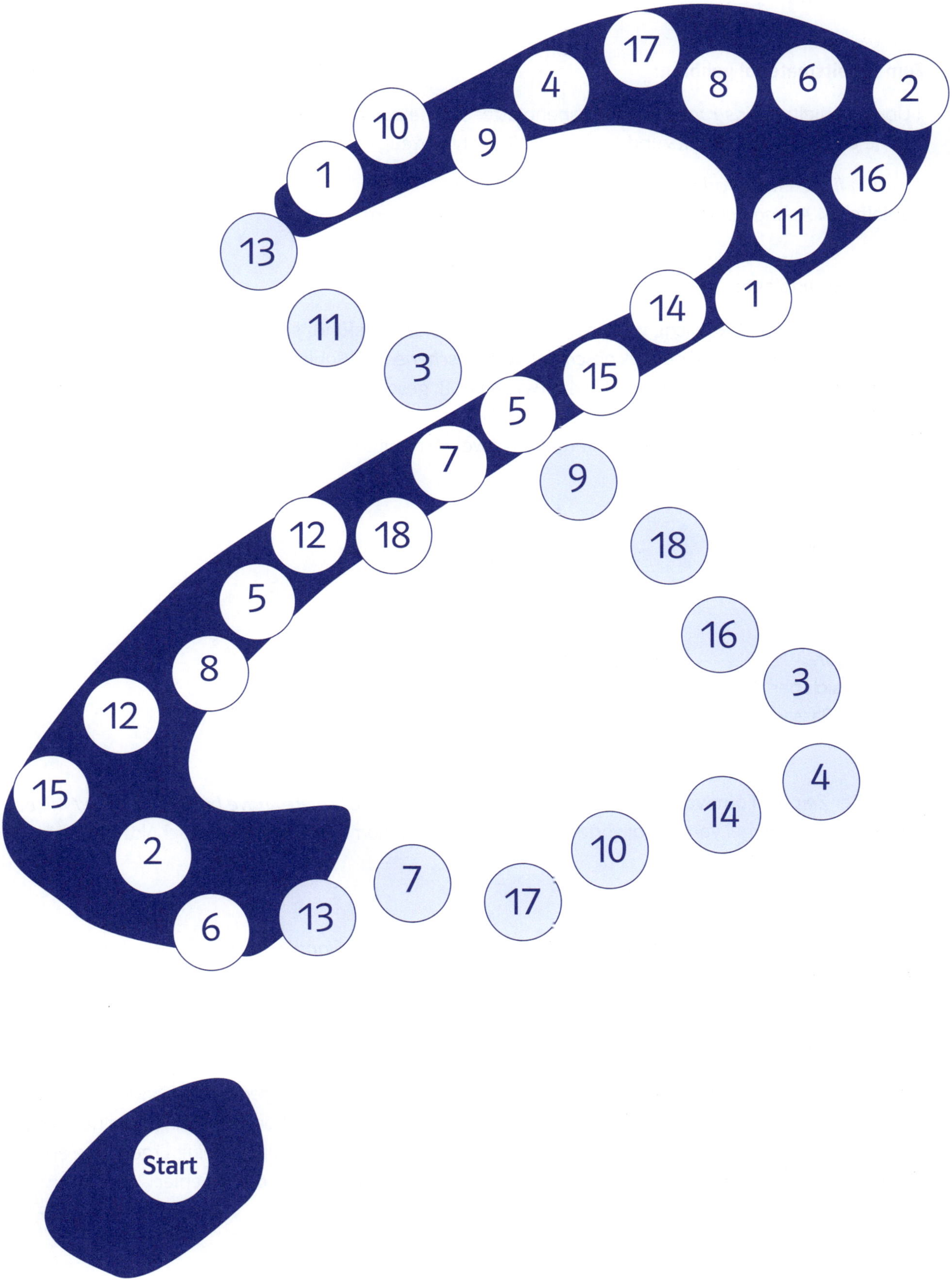



ISBN: 978-3-12-581180-5

# 5a The passive

## Instructions

### Zum Arbeitsmaterial gehören:

1 Übungsanleitung *Instructions*, 2 Aufgabenblätter *5a The passive Task 1* und *Task 2*, 2 separate Lösungsblätter *5a The passive Task 1: results* und *Task 2: results*, Schreibzeug

Für *mündliche Partnerarbeit* benötigt man zusätzlich:
1 Spielfeld *4 Asking questions*, 1 Spielfigur, 1 Würfel (1–6 Augen)

### 1. Übungsgrundlage:

Passivsätze beschreiben nicht, wer oder was eine Handlung ausführt, sondern stellen die *Person oder Sache* in den Vordergrund, mit der *etwas geschieht* oder *geschehen ist*. Subjekt des Passivsatzes ist also jemand oder etwas, mit dem etwas *getan wird*. Diesem *werden* (z. B. gesehen / geputzt / beschädigt / verletzt … werden) entspricht im Englischen das Verb *be*.
So besteht die Passivform des Verbs immer aus zwei Elementen:

| Form von *be* | + | Grundform + *ed*<br>*3. Form* des Verbs |
|---|---|---|
| Die Form von *be* ist *veränderbar*.<br>Sie passt sich der *Zeit* an, in der das Passiv stehen muss. | | Dieser Teil ist *immer gleich*:<br>bei regelmäßigen Verben:<br>**Gf + *ed***<br>bei unregelmäßigen Verben:<br>***3. Form*** |

In welcher *Zeit* die Form von *be* stehen muss (ob *am / is / are / was / were / have been / has been / will be …*), das hängt in der Regel von *Signalwörtern* ab, die im Satz vorkommen – genau wie bei Aktivsätzen.

### 2. Übungsziel:

Die Schüler haben die Aufgabe, entsprechend der vorgegebenen *Signalwörter* die richtigen *Passivformen* der Verben in den Klammern einzusetzen.

### 3. a) Schriftliche Übungsweise (Stillarbeit):

Aufgabe 5a ist als *schriftliche Übung* gedacht. Alle Sätze enthalten *kursiv gedruckte Signalwörter*. Sie legen fest, in welcher *Zeit* der Passivsatz stehen muss. Achte also auf die Signalwörter, ordne ihnen die richtige Zeit zu und setze die *Verben in Klammern* in die entsprechenden *Passivformen*. Vergleiche deine Ergebnisse anschließend mit den Lösungsblättern *Task 1: results* bzw. *Task 2: results* und berichtige deine Fehler.


Grammar Tandem Activities
ISBN: 978-3-12-581180-5

**b) Mündliche Partnerarbeit:**

Aufgabe 5a ist auch als *mündliche Partnerarbeit* möglich. Dabei bearbeitet Partner A das Aufgabenblatt *5a The passive Task 1* und Partner B bearbeitet *Task 2*. Beide Partner benutzen das Spielfeld zu *4 Asking questions* und dieselbe Spielfigur. Sie beginnen bei *Start* und folgen dem *Fragezeichen*, indem sie stets um die gewürfelte Augenzahl vorrücken. Ab der zweiten Runde (es können beliebig viele gespielt werden) wird das Feld *Start* einfach ausgelassen.
Den Zahlen von 1–18, die auf dem Spielfeld doppelt vorkommen, ist auf jedem Aufgabenblatt jeweils *ein Passivsatz* zugeordnet. Landet die Spielfigur zum Beispiel auf Feld 8, so vervollständigt der Spieler, der soeben gewürfelt hat, Satz 8 auf seinem Aufgabenblatt mit der dazugehörigen *Passivform des Verbs in Klammern*.

So vermeidet man Fehler:

- Achte auf die *kursiv gedruckten Signalwörter*. Sie legen fest, in welcher *Zeit* der Passivsatz stehen muss.
- Ordne den Signalwörtern *die richtige Zeit* zu.
- Setze die *Verben in Klammern* in die entsprechenden *Passivformen*.
- Beide Partner *korrigieren sich gegenseitig*. (Die Lösungen sind jeweils auf der Rückseite des Aufgabenblatts des Partners aufgelistet.)

Soll die Übung Wettspielcharakter haben, so erhält jeder Partner pro richtig gebildeten Passivsatz *einen Punkt / Strich*, der auf einem Extrablatt notiert wird. Wer am Übungsende die meisten Punkte / Striche gesammelt hat, ist Sieger.

Grammar Tandem Activities
ISBN: 978-3-12-581180-5

## 5 a The passive: Task 1

1. The World Trade Center ______________ *in the 1970s* and ______________ *in 2001* by terrorists. (build / destroy)
2. Only a few tickets for the concert ______________ *so far*. (sell)
3. Bags and suitcases ______________ *always* ______________ before the flight. (check)
4. People in California hope that San Francisco ______________ by an earthquake *in the near future*. (not hit)
5. *Today* only few stars ______________ by somebody who plans their career. (not manage)
6. *Yesterday* Jack suddenly appeared at a party although he ______________ . (not invite)

7. ______________ Uncle Alan ______________ at the hospital *tomorrow*? (examine)
8. Books on the bestseller list ______________ *often* ______________ into different languages. (translate)
9. Julie ______________ some extra work for talking in class *some days ago*. (give)
10. If you buy something on the Internet, it ______________ *usually* ______________ for before you get it. (must pay)
11. Fewer people ______________ in road accidents *last year*. (kill)
12. *On Saturdays* Mr Benson ______________ by his alarm clock – he sleeps late! (not wake up)

13. Most pupils ______________ to school by bus *every morning*. (take)
14. The bank robbers ______________ , because they wore masks during *yesterday's* raid. (not recognize)
15. *Today* van Gogh's pictures ______________ by anybody who isn't a millionaire. (can't buy)
16. A citizens' meeting ______________ in the town hall *once a year*. (hold)
17. *In 1848* gold ______________ in California and lots of adventurers moved west. (find)
18. ______________ the two gangsters *already* ______________ by the police? (catch)


Grammar Tandem Activities
ISBN: 978-3-12-581180-5

Klett

## 5a The passive: Task 2 (results)

1. Internet pages *are* often *written* in English because English is a world language.
2. A lot of buildings, bridges and roads *were damaged* in yesterday's earthquake.
3. Maybe astronauts *will be sent* on a trip to Mars in 2050.
4. Mrs Dean usually does the cooking, but at the weekends lunch *is cooked* by her husband.
5. Today mobile phones *mustn't be used* at school during lessons and breaks.
6. Two of Tommy's silly mistakes *weren't noticed* by his English teacher in the test last week.

7. Our team *wasn't beaten* although they played badly two days ago.
8. It is true that a lot of energy *could be saved* if we tried hard.
9. Even today millions of children *aren't taught* how to read and write.
10. *Have* you ever *been kissed* by a boyfriend or girlfriend?
11. A lot of unemployed people feel day by day that they *aren't needed* any more.
12. Last Monday morning the bank manager couldn't believe his eyes: the safe *was broken open* and all the money *was stolen*!

13. It is always an experienced player of the team who *is chosen* as captain.
14. The roadworks *won't be finished* before next summer.
15. Did you know that President John F. Kennedy *was shot* in Dallas in 1963?
16. What a strange guest! He *hasn't been seen* by anybody since his arrival.
17. Yesterday's accident happened because a lorry *was overtaken* on an icy road.
18. Every four years Hannah's birthday *is celebrated* with a big party because it is on 29th February.

Every four years Hannah's birthday *is celebrated* with a big party.

**Form von *be*** + **Grundform + *ed***
***3. Form* des Verbs**

Grammar Tandem Activities
ISBN: 978-3-12-581180-5

## 5a The passive: Task 2

1. Internet pages ___________ *often* ___________________ in English because English is a world language. (write)
2. A lot of buildings, bridges and roads ___________________________ in *yesterday's* earthquake. (damage)
3. Maybe astronauts ___________________________ on a trip to Mars *in 2050*. (send)
4. Mrs Dean usually does the cooking, but *at the weekends* lunch ____________________ by her husband. (cook)
5. *Today* mobile phones ______________________ at school during lessons and breaks. (mustn't use)
6. Two of Tommy's silly mistakes _______________________ by his English teacher in the test *last week*. (not notice)

7. Our team _________________________ although they played badly *two days ago*. (not beat)
8. It is true that a lot of energy _________________________________ *if* we tried hard. (can save)
9. Even *today* millions of children ____________________________ how to read and write. (not teach)
10. ___________ you *ever* ______________________ by a boyfriend or girlfriend? (kiss)
11. A lot of unemployed people feel *day by day* that they _________________________ any more. (not need)
12. *Last Monday morning* the bank manager couldn't believe his eyes: the safe _______________________ and all the money ____________________ ! (break open / steal)

13. It is *always* an experienced player of the team who ______________________ as captain. (choose)
14. The roadworks ______________________ before *next summer*. (not finish)
15. Did you know that President John F. Kennedy _____________________ in Dallas *in 1963*? (shoot)
16. What a strange guest! He ___________________________ by anybody *since* his arrival. (not see)
17. *Yesterday's* accident happened because a lorry _______________________ on an icy road. (overtake)
18. *Every four years* Hannah's birthday ____________________________ with a big party because it is on 29th February. (celebrate)


Grammar Tandem Activities
ISBN: 978-3-12-581180-5

## 5a The passive: Task 1 (results)

1. The World Trade Center *was built* in the 1970s and *(was) destroyed* in 2001 by terrorists.
2. Only a few tickets for the concert *have been sold* so far.
3. Bags and suitcases *are* always *checked* before the flight.
4. People in California hope that San Francisco *won't be hit* by an earthquake in the near future.
5. Today only few stars *aren't managed* by somebody who plans their career.
6. Yesterday Jack suddenly appeared at a party although he *wasn't invited*. (Yesterday Jack suddenly appeared at a party although he *hadn't been invited*.)

7. *Will* Uncle Alan *be examined* at the hospital tomorrow?
8. Books on the bestseller list *are* often *translated* into different languages.
9. Julie *was given* some extra work for talking in class some days ago.
10. If you buy something on the Internet, it *must* usually *be paid* for before you get it.
11. Fewer people *were killed* in road accidents last year.
12. On Saturdays Mr Benson *isn't woken up* by his alarm clock – he sleeps late!

13. Most pupils *are taken* to school by bus every morning.
14. The bank robbers *weren't recognized*, because they wore masks during yesterday's raid.
15. Today van Gogh's pictures *can't be bought* by anybody who isn't a millionaire.
16. A citizens' meeting *is held* in the town hall once a year.
17. In 1848 gold *was found* in California and lots of adventurers moved west.
18. *Have* the two gangsters already *been caught* by the police?

Most pupils *are taken* to school by bus.

**Form von *be*** + **Grundform + *ed*** / ***3. Form* des Verbs**


ISBN: 978-3-12-581180-5

# 5b The passive

## Instructions

### Zum Arbeitsmaterial gehören:

1 Übungsanleitung *Instructions*, je 1 Aufgabenblatt *5b The passive* für Partner A und Partner B, je 1 Lösungsblatt *5b The passive Partner A: results* und *Partner B: results*, 2 verschiedenfarbige Würfel (1–6 Augen)

### 1. Übungsgrundlage:

Passivsätze beschreiben nicht, wer oder was eine Handlung ausführt, sondern stellen die *Person oder Sache* in den Vordergrund, mit der *etwas geschieht* oder *geschehen ist*. Subjekt des Passivsatzes ist also jemand oder etwas, mit dem etwas *getan wird*. Diesem *werden* (z. B. gesehen / geputzt / beschädigt / verletzt ... werden) entspricht im Englischen das Verb *be*. So besteht die *Passivform des Verbs* immer aus *zwei Elementen*:

| Form von *be* | + | Grundform + *ed*<br>*3. Form* des Verbs |
|---|---|---|
| Die Form von *be* ist *veränderbar*.<br>Sie passt sich der *Zeit* an, in der das Passiv stehen muss. | | Dieser Teil ist *immer gleich*:<br>bei regelmäßigen Verben:<br>**Gf + *ed***<br>bei unregelmäßigen Verben:<br>***3. Form*** |

In welcher *Zeit* die Form von *be* stehen muss (ob *am / is / are / was / were / have been / has been / will be ...*), das hängt in der Regel von *Signalwörtern* ab, die im Satz vorkommen – genau wie bei Aktivsätzen.

### 2. Übungsziel:

Anhand des Arbeitsmaterials soll geübt werden, mit Hilfe von *Satzbausteinen* eigene Passivsätze zu bilden.

### 3. Übungsweise:

Aufgabe 5b ist auf *mündliche Partnerarbeit* hin angelegt. Zuerst legen beide Partner fest, welcher Würfel die *Zehner* bzw. die *Einer* angibt. Dann würfeln sie *abwechselnd* Zahlen zwischen 11 und 66 aus.
Dabei bildet der Partner, auf dessen Aufgabenblatt sich die ausgewürfelte Zahl befindet, mit Hilfe der Bausteine aus den vier Spalten den jeweiligen Passivsatz.
So gelingt das:

- Zuerst die ... *when-Spalte* lesen. Sie enthält die Signalwörter.
- Den Signalwörtern die entsprechende Zeit zuordnen.
- Die Begriffe aus den vier Spalten der Reihe nach *von links nach rechts* miteinander verbinden. Vorsicht! Das Verb muss dabei *ins Passiv* gesetzt werden.
- Bitte die *Satzstellung* beachten. (Nicht alle Signalwörter dürfen am Satzende stehen.)
- Beide Partner *korrigieren sich gegenseitig*. (Auf jedem Aufgabenblatt sind die Lösungen des Partners auf der Rückseite aufgelistet.)

Soll die Übung Wettspielcharakter haben, so erhält jeder Partner pro richtigen Passivsatz *einen Punkt / Strich*, der auf einem Extrablatt notiert wird. Wer am Übungsende die meisten Punkte / Striche gesammelt hat, ist Sieger.


ISBN: 978-3-12-581180-5

## 5 b The passive: Partner A

| | ... what / who? | verb / action | ... where | ... when? |
|---|---|---|---|---|
| 11 | some great CDs | bring out | in America | last month |
| 12 | many new films | not make | in Hollywood | today |
| 13 | a dog | should take out | for a walk | every day |
| 14 | the old houses | pull down | in the city centre | already |
| 15 | a sports bag and an umbrella | leave | on the school bus | the day before yesterday |
| 16 | economical cars | use | in most countries | in the future |
| 21 | fresh vegetables and fruit | sell | at the market | twice a week |
| 22 | the pilot of the sports aircraft | not kill | in the plane crash | yesterday |
| 23 | Tim and Alex | needn't drive | to football training | today |
| 24 | a new heating system | install | in our old house | two weeks ago |
| 25 | a big supermarket | open | in my neighbourhood | just |
| 26 | German | not teach | at British schools | usually |
| 31 | old Mrs Hepburn | not see | outside of her house | since her operation |
| 32 | lots of black slaves | transport | from Africa to America | in the 17th century |
| 33 | many jobs | offer | in daily newspapers | on Saturdays |
| 34 | my broken bike | repair | at the bicycle shop | tomorrow |
| 35 | the wreck of the Titanic | find | at the bottom of the sea | in 1985 |
| 36 | a lot of tropical rain forest | destroy | in Brazil | every year |

Grammar Tandem Activities
ISBN: 978-3-12-581180-5

## 5 b The passive: Partner B (results)

**41** A million copies of the new CD *have been sold* worldwide so far.

**42** Father's new car *was damaged* in a car accident two days ago.

**43** A conference on new technologies *will be held* in Tokyo next Thursday.

**44** The first car with a petrol engine *was built* in Germany in 1885.

**45** More energy *must be saved* in private households in the future.

**46** Traffic jams *aren't expected* on German motorways at the weekend.

**51** German tourists *can be met* almost everywhere in summer.

**52** English *is spoken* all over the world today.

**53** Sina and Toby *weren't invited* to Emily's party last weekend.

**54** Somebody *is shot* in cities like Chicago every night.

**55** This programme *is shown* on TV on Sundays.

**56** Dangerous industrial waste *was carried* to Third World countries in the past.

**61** An expensive bike *was stolen* at the station yesterday.

**62** Careless tourists *are* sometimes *attacked and killed* in safari parks.

**63** Petrol-driven vehicles *won't be used* in Germany any longer in fifty years.

**64** Lazy pupils *were beaten* at school a century ago.

**65** The dangers of terrorism *have been discussed* in books and films since 11th September, 2001.

**66** Wages and salaries *are paid* here in Germany once a month.

---

**Examples**

| | | | |
|---|---|---|---|
| meals<br>they | cook<br>put | on an open fire<br>in the microwave | two centuries ago<br>today |

Meals *were cooked* on an open fire two centuries ago.
They *are put* in the microwave today.

Grammar Tandem Activities
ISBN: 978-3-12-581180-5

## 5 b The passive: Partner B

| | ... what / who? | verb / action | ... where | ... when? |
|---|---|---|---|---|
| 41 | a million copies of the new CD | sell | worldwide | so far |
| 42 | father's new car | damage | in a car accident | two days ago |
| 43 | a conference on new technologies | hold | in Tokyo | next Thursday |
| 44 | the first car with a petrol engine | build | in Germany | in 1885 |
| 45 | more energy | must save | in private households | in the future |
| 46 | traffic jams | not expect | on German motorways | at the weekend |
| 51 | German tourists | can meet | almost everywhere | in summer |
| 52 | English | speak | all over the world | today |
| 53 | Sina and Toby | not invite | to Emily's party | last weekend |
| 54 | somebody | shoot | in cities like Chicago | every night |
| 55 | this programme | show | on TV | on Sundays |
| 56 | dangerous industrial waste | carry | to Third World countries | in the past |
| 61 | an expensive bike | steal | at the station | yesterday |
| 62 | careless tourists | attack and kill | in safari parks | sometimes |
| 63 | petrol-driven vehicles | not use | in Germany any longer | in fifty years |
| 64 | lazy pupils | beat | at school | a century ago |
| 65 | the dangers of terrorism | discuss | in books and films | since 11th September, 2001 |
| 66 | wages and salaries | pay | here in Germany | once a month |

Grammar Tandem Activities
ISBN: 978-3-12-581180-5

## 5 b The passive: Partner A (results)

**11** Some great CDs *were brought out* in America last month.

**12** Many new films *aren't made* in Hollywood today.

**13** A dog *should be taken out* for a walk every day.

**14** The old houses *have* already *been pulled down* in the city centre.

**15** A sports bag and an umbrella *were left* on the school bus the day before yesterday.

**16** Economical cars *will be used* in most countries in the future.

**21** Fresh vegetables and fruit *are sold* at the market twice a week.

**22** The pilot of the sports aircraft *wasn't killed* in the plane crash yesterday.

**23** Tim and Alex *needn't be driven* to football training today.

**24** A new heating system *was installed* in our old house two weeks ago.

**25** A big supermarket *has* just *been opened* in my neighbourhood.

**26** German *isn't* usually *taught* at British schools. (Usually German *isn't taught* at British schools.)

**31** Old Mrs Hepburn *hasn't been seen* outside of her house since her operation.

**32** Lots of black slaves *were transported* from Africa to America in the 17th century.

**33** Many jobs *are offered* in daily newspapers on Saturdays.

**34** My broken bike *will be repaired* at the bicycle shop tomorrow.

**35** The wreck of the Titanic *was found* at the bottom of the sea in 1985.

**36** A lot of tropical rain forest *is destroyed* in Brazil every year.

---

**Examples**

| | | | |
|---|---|---|---|
| pandas<br>they | hunt<br>protect | in China<br>everywhere | for many years<br>today |

Pandas *have been hunted* in China for many years.
They *are protected* everywhere today.

Grammar Tandem Activities
ISBN: 978-3-12-581180-5

# 5c The passive

## Instructions

### Zum Arbeitsmaterial gehören:

1 Übungsanleitung *Instructions*, je 1 Aufgabenblatt *5c The passive* für Partner A und Partner B mit den Lösungen (*results*) des Partners, 1 Farbwürfel (gelb, rot, blau, grün, weiß, schwarz), 1 Würfel (1–6 Augen)

### 1. Übungsgrundlage:

Passivsätze beschreiben nicht, wer oder was eine Handlung ausführt, sondern stellen die *Person oder Sache* in den Vordergrund, mit der *etwas geschieht* oder *geschehen ist*. Subjekt des Passivsatzes ist also jemand oder etwas, mit dem etwas *getan wird*. Diesem *werden* (z. B. gesehen / geputzt / beschädigt / verletzt … werden) entspricht im Englischen das Verb *be*.
So besteht die *Passivform des Verbs* immer aus *zwei Elementen*:

| Form von *be* | + | Grundform + *ed*<br>*3. Form* des Verbs |
| --- | --- | --- |
| Die Form von *be* ist *veränderbar*.<br>Sie passt sich der *Zeit* an, in der das Passiv stehen muss. | | Dieser Teil ist *immer gleich*:<br>bei regelmäßigen Verben:<br>**Gf + *ed***<br>bei unregelmäßigen Verben:<br>***3. Form*** |

In welcher *Zeit* die Form von *be* stehen muss (ob *am / is / are / was / were / have been / has been / will be …*), das hängt in der Regel von *Signalwörtern* ab, die im Satz vorkommen – genau wie bei Aktivsätzen.

Wenn wie bei Aufgabe 5c *ganze Sätze* vom Aktiv ins Passiv gesetzt werden sollen, rückt die Person / Sache in den Vordergrund, mit der etwas *getan wird*. Sie rückt auch im Passivsatz *nach vorne* und wird zum *Subjekt*.

Wie das Wappen als „Eselsbrücke" veranschaulicht, wird praktisch der ganze Satz *auf den Kopf* gestellt: das **O**bjekt aus dem Aktivsatz wird (wie die Schwerter auf den Wappen veranschaulichen) zum neuen **S**ubjekt im Passivsatz – und umgekehrt. Gleichzeitig muss aber das *Verb* durch die entsprechende *Form von be* in die *Passivform* gesetzt werden.

ISBN: 978-3-12-581180-5

Hierzu ein Beispiel:

***Many doctors*** wear ***masks and rubber gloves*** at work.

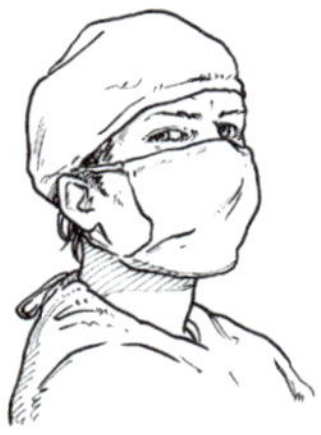

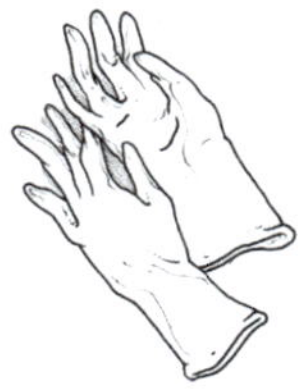

***Masks and rubber gloves*** *are worn* at work ***by many doctors***.

### 2. Übungsziel:

Mit dem Arbeitsmaterial soll geübt werden, einfache Sätze aus dem *Aktiv ins Passiv* zu setzen.

### 3. Übungsweise:

Aufgabe 5c ist auf *mündliche Partnerarbeit* hin angelegt. Die beiden Partner würfeln *abwechselnd eine Farb-Zahl-Kombination* aus (z. B. grün 4). Derjenige Partner, auf dessen Aufgabenblatt sich die ausgewürfelte Kombination befindet, setzt den entsprechenden Aktivsatz ins Passiv. Die Zeit als solche bleibt erhalten, muss jedoch ins Passiv gesetzt werden. Das Wappen als „Eselsbrücke" erleichtert die ganze Aufgabe ungemein. Doch Vorsicht – der *letzte Teil* des Aktivsatzes ist *nicht immer das Objekt*, das nach vorne kommt und zum Subjekt wird!

- Beide Partner *korrigieren sich gegenseitig*. (Unten auf jedem Aufgabenblatt sind die Lösungen des Partners aufgelistet.)

Soll die Übung Wettspielcharakter haben, so erhält jeder Partner pro richtigen Passivsatz *einen Punkt / Strich*, der auf einem Extrablatt notiert wird. Wer am Übungsende die meisten Punkte / Striche gesammelt hat, ist Sieger.


Grammar Tandem Activities
ISBN: 978-3-12-581180-5

## 5c The passive: Partner A

| (1–6 yellow) | | |
|---|---|---|
| 1 | The Japanese *make* the best cameras in the world. | |
| 2 | Store detectives *can watch* thieves on video cameras. | |
| 3 | Bad weather *forced* the mountain climbers to turn back. | |
| 4 | A responsible shop assistant *doesn't sell* alcohol to children. | |
| 5 | The doctor *hasn't examined* her yet. | |
| 6 | The teacher *will describe* the project in our next lesson. | |

| (1–6 red) | |
|---|---|
| 1 | The pupils *left* the classroom in a complete mess. |
| 2 | A hungry bear *had smelt* the campers' food. |
| 3 | The doctors *didn't notice* his serious illness. |
| 4 | The police *won't give* details about the crime. |
| 5 | The weather forecast *expects* heavy rainfall. |
| 6 | German pupils *mustn't use* dictionaries in the English exam. |

| (1–6 blue) | |
|---|---|
| 1 | Many European countries *introduced* the euro in 2002. |
| 2 | Engineers *had checked* the plane just before the crash. |
| 3 | My mother *wakes* me *up* at half past six. |
| 4 | Heavy thunderstorms *have killed* three people. |
| 5 | Parents *should put* little children to bed early. |
| 6 | A lot of tourists *buy* cheap souvenirs. |

---

## 5c The passive: Partner B (results)

(green)

1 Late at night the Millers *were woken up* by a loud noise.
2 The whole village *has been shaken* by the terrible news.
3 The effects of climate change *can't be stopped* by one single state.
4 New vocabulary *is introduced* in English by most teachers.
5 A new pizzeria *will be opened* next month (by Mr and Mrs Rizza).
6 He *was chosen* as 'Footballer of the Year' by a sports magazine.

(white)

1 The national park visitors *had been warned* of bears (by a big sign).
2 Huge jumbo jets *aren't flown* by pilots with little experience.
3 Our new museum of art *will be visited* by millions of art lovers.
4 The kidnapper *hasn't been caught* yet (by police officers).
5 The tourists *were informed* about the sights of the city (by a guide).
6 These old football boots *won't be used* any more (by my father).

(black)

1 On New Year's Eve millions *are spent* on fireworks (by Germans).
2 One of the drivers *was taken* to the nearest hospital (by an ambulance).
3 The explosion *could be heard* (by people) in the neighbouring town.
4 The star player *was interviewed* after the match (by a TV reporter).
5 An exciting match *is expected* today (by the fans of both teams).
6 All the washing-up *had been done* by the guests themselves.

Grammar Tandem Activities
ISBN: 978-3-12-581180-5

## 5c The passive: Partner B

(1–6 green)

| | |
|---|---|
| 1 | Late at night a loud noise *woke* the Millers *up*. |
| 2 | The terrible news *has shaken* the whole village. |
| 3 | One single state *can't stop* the effects of climate change. |
| 4 | Most teachers *introduce* new vocabulary in English. |
| 5 | Mr and Mrs Rizza *will open* a new pizzeria next month. |
| 6 | A sports magazine *chose* him as 'Footballer of the Year'. |

(1–6 white)

| | |
|---|---|
| 1 | A big sign *had warned* the national park visitors of bears. |
| 2 | Pilots with little experience *don't fly* huge jumbo jets. |
| 3 | Millions of art lovers *will visit* our new museum of art. |
| 4 | Police officers *haven't caught* the kidnapper yet. |
| 5 | A guide *informed* the tourists about the sights of the city. |
| 6 | My father *won't use* these old football boots any more. |

(1–6 black)

| | |
|---|---|
| 1 | On New Year's Eve Germans *spend* millions on fireworks. |
| 2 | An ambulance *took* one of the drivers to the nearest hospital. |
| 3 | People in the neighbouring town *could hear* the explosion. |
| 4 | A TV reporter *interviewed* the star player after the match. |
| 5 | The fans of both teams *expect* an exciting match today. |
| 6 | The guests themselves *had done* all the washing-up. |

## 5c The passive: Partner A (results)

(yellow)

1 The best cameras in the world *are made* by the Japanese.
2 Thieves *can be watched* on video cameras (by store detectives).
3 The mountain climbers *were forced* to turn back by bad weather.
4 Alcohol *isn't sold* to children (by a responsible shop assistant).
5 She *hasn't been examined* yet by the doctor.
6 The project *will be described* in our next lesson (by the teacher).

(red)

1 The classroom *was left* (by the pupils) in a complete mess.
2 The campers' food *had been smelt* by a hungry bear.
3 His serious illness *wasn't noticed* by the doctors.
4 Details about the crime *won't be given* (by the police).
5 Heavy rainfall *is expected* by the weather forecast.
6 Dictionaries *mustn't be used* in the English exam (by German pupils).

(blue)

1 The euro *was introduced* in 2002 by many European countries.
2 The plane *had been checked* (by engineers) just before the crash.
3 I *am woken up* at half past six (by my mother).
4 Three people *have been killed* by heavy thunderstorms.
5 Little children *should be put* to bed early (by parents).
6 Cheap souvenirs *are bought* by a lot of tourists.


Grammar Tandem Activities
ISBN: 978-3-12-581180-5

# 6abc Reported speech

## Instructions

### Zum Arbeitsmaterial gehören:

1 Übungsanleitung *Instructions*, 1 gemeinsames Aufgabenblatt *Reported speech* für Partner A (Ziffern 11–36) und Partner B (Ziffern 41–66) in einer der Versionen *6a*, *6b* oder *6c*, je 1 Lösungsblatt *Reported speech Partner A: results* und *Partner B: results* in den entsprechenden Versionen *6a*, *6b* oder *6c*, 2 verschiedenfarbige Würfel (1–6 Augen)

### 1. Übungsgrundlage:

In der indirekten Rede wird wiedergegeben, was jemand *gerade sagt* (Dolmetschen) oder *gesagt hat* (wenn zu einem späteren Zeitpunkt berichtet wird). Wird über etwas berichtet, was *in einem vergangenen Zeitraum* gesagt wurde, dann steht das Verb im Einleitungssatz der direkten Rede im *simple past* (z. B. bei He <u>said</u>: "… ." / She <u>asked</u>: "Do / Does … ?" / They <u>wanted</u> to know: "Why … ?").

Für den Einleitungssatz ändert sich in der *indirekten Rede* nichts (He <u>said</u> (that) … . / She <u>asked</u> if / whether … . / They <u>wanted</u> to know why … .). In der *indirekten Rede selbst*, die auf den Einleitungssatz folgt, ändern sich jedoch *die Zeiten* der Verben.
Sie werden um *eine Zeitstufe* in die Vergangenheit *zurückverschoben* (= backshift of tenses), z. B. wird aus dem *simple past* das *past perfect*.

Auch andere Angaben müssen dem *Berichterstatter* und dem *Ort* (von wo aus) und der *Zeit* (zu der er berichtet) angepasst werden. Es sind eine Reihe von Veränderungen notwendig, die hier nur angedeutet werden können. Die Arbeit mit dem Übungsmaterial bedarf also der vorherigen Wiederholung oder Bewusstmachung der Regeln. Hier ein Beispiel für diese Veränderungen:

Mrs Lawrence said:

Mrs Lawrence **said** *(that) the* year *before they had had* a terrible hurricane *there* in Florida.

### 2. Übungsziel:

Durch die Übung mit dem Arbeitsmaterial sollen die Schüler bei der Übertragung von *statements* (Aussagesätzen), *questions* (Fragen) und *commands* (Aufforderungen) von der direkten in die indirekte Rede eine gewisse Routine erlangen.


ISBN: 978-3-12-581180-5

### 3. Übungsweise:

Die Aufgaben 6abc sind auf *mündliche Partnerarbeit* hin angelegt. Beide Partner *sitzen einander am Tisch gegenüber*. Das gemeinsame Aufgabenblatt liegt so vor ihnen, dass jeder eine Seitenhälfte lesen und bearbeiten kann. Somit ist klar, wer Partner A und wer Partner B ist. Nun wird bestimmt, welcher Würfel die *Zehner* bzw. die *Einer* angibt. Dann würfeln beide Partner *abwechselnd* Zahlen zwischen 11 und 66 aus. Dabei setzt der Partner, auf dessen *Seitenhälfte* sich die gewürfelte Zahl befindet, die jeweilige Aufgabe in die *indirekte Rede*. Dazu sollte er sich vergewissern:

- Handelt es sich um eine *Aussage, Frage* oder *Aufforderung*?
- Welche *Zeit* steht in der *direkten* Rede?
- Welche *Zeit* ergibt sich daraus für die *indirekte* Rede?
- Wie ändern sich *Personalpronomen (I, you …), Possessivpronomen (my, your …)* bzw. *Orts-* und *Zeitangaben*?
- Beide Partner *korrigieren sich gegenseitig*. (Jeder benötigt dazu das Lösungsblatt mit den Ziffern seines Partners.)

Es empfiehlt sich, dass Partner A und B zu gegebener Zeit ihre Rollen tauschen, indem sie das Aufgabenblatt drehen und die Lösungsblätter austauschen.

Soll die Übung Wettspielcharakter haben, so erhält jeder Partner für eine richtige Übertragung in die indirekte Rede *zwei Punkte / Striche*, die auf einem Extrablatt notiert werden. Wer am Übungsende die meisten Punkte / Striche gesammelt hat, ist Sieger.

### 4. Kombination von Aufgabenblättern:

Wenn Sie die Aufgaben von *6a, Partner A* und *6b, Partner B* entsprechend auf **ein** *Aufgabenblatt* kopieren, dann kann Ihre Klasse auch ausschließlich *Statements* üben. Umgekehrt können *Questions und commands* auch isoliert bearbeitet werden, wenn Sie *6a, Partner B* und *6b, Partner A* miteinander kombinieren.

Vergessen Sie jedoch nicht, die veränderte Aufgabenstellung bei der Zuteilung der *Lösungsblätter* für die gegenseitige Ergebniskontrolle zu berücksichtigen.


Grammar Tandem Activities
ISBN: 978-3-12-581180-5

## 6a Reported speech: Partner A (Statements)

| | |
|---|---|
| 11 | Mother told me: "You will be late if you don't hurry." |
| 12 | The boy told the store detective: "I haven't stolen anything." |
| 13 | The waiter replied: "We don't sell alcoholic drinks to under-eighteens." |
| 14 | The driver remarked: "We drove so fast because we were in a hurry." |
| 15 | Jo explained: "Sally has stayed at home because she hates crowded discos." |
| 16 | Little Bill told his friend Tina: "I have no idea where your ball can be." |
| 21 | Melanie remarked: "I didn't buy it because it was too expensive." |
| 22 | The old lady told the doctor: "I'm feeling much better than yesterday." |
| 23 | The police reported: "A child saw the criminals as they hid the money." |
| 24 | Sue explained: "I can't babysit tonight because I have to do my homework." |
| 25 | Mrs Ross told her daughter: "You won't find a job that is only fun." |
| 26 | My parents said: "The weather always changes when our holiday has begun." |
| 31 | Grandfather said: "I got off at Hull because I had forgotten to change trains." |
| 32 | Before the concert Chris said: "I hope they will play my favourite songs." |
| 33 | They told the teacher: "We aren't just talking – we are discussing the topic." |
| 34 | Mr Shaw pointed out: "Pupils aren't allowed to eat in my lessons." |
| 35 | Grandma went on: "I didn't sleep well last night because I had a crazy dream." |
| 36 | One of the protesters told the reporter: "War doesn't solve any problems." |

## 6a Reported speech: Partner B (Questions and commands)

| | |
|---|---|
| 41 | Mrs Mason asked her brother Elliot: „Why didn't you ask me for help?" |
| 42 | She wanted to know from her boss: „Do I have to work on Saturdays, too?" |
| 43 | The teacher asked: „Has everybody done the exercises for today?" |
| 44 | The young man asked: „How much are the trainers in the shop window?" |
| 45 | My friends wanted to know: „Did Germany win the football match?" |
| 46 | The teacher asked his pupils: „Do you read any newspapers?" |
| 51 | Ron and Joe asked the girls: „Who are you waiting for?" |
| 52 | All the pupils asked Mrs Hunt: „Why haven't you corrected our tests yet?" |
| 53 | After the job interview Jane wondered: „Will I really get this job?" |
| 54 | Mrs McLean looked up to the sky and wondered: „Is it going to rain?" |
| 55 | Mr Hilton wanted to know angrily: „Why can't you stop talking, Simon?" |
| 56 | Lynn and Victoria asked the new boy: „What did you do last weekend?" |
| 61 | Mrs Taylor told her children: „Wash your hands before you sit down." |
| 62 | Doctor Brown advised his patients: „Don't smoke, and do more sport." |
| 63 | Mr Clark ordered some boys: „Don't kick the ball into my garden." |
| 64 | Little Kitty asked her mother: „Give me an apple, please." |
| 65 | The English teacher told some pupils: „Don't be so lazy!" |
| 66 | Mrs Powell told her son: „Please lay the table." |

Grammar Tandem Activities
ISBN: 978-3-12-581180-5

# 6a Reported speech: Partner A (results)

**11** Mother told me (that) I / we would be late if I / we didn't hurry.

**12** The boy told the store detective (that) he hadn't stolen anything.

**13** The waiter replied (that) they didn't sell alcoholic drinks to under-eighteens.

**14** The driver remarked (that) they had driven so fast because they had been in a hurry.

**15** Jo explained (that) Sally had stayed at home because she hated crowded discos.

**16** Little Bill told his friend Tina (that) he had no idea where her ball could be.

**21** Melanie remarked (that) she hadn't bought it because it had been too expensive.

**22** The old lady told the doctor (that) she was feeling much better than the day before.

**23** The police reported (that) a child had seen the criminals as they had hidden the money.

**24** Sue explained (that) she couldn't babysit that night because she had to do her homework.

**25** Mrs Ross told her daughter (that) she wouldn't find a job that was only fun.

**26** My parents said (that) the weather always changed when our / their holiday had begun.

**31** Grandfather said (that) he had got off at Hull because he had forgotten to change trains.

**32** Before the concert Chris said (that) he hoped they would play his favourite songs.

**33** They told the teacher (that) they weren't just talking – they were discussing the topic.

**34** Mr Shaw pointed out (that) pupils weren't allowed to eat in his lessons.

**35** Grandma went on (that) she hadn't slept well the night before because she had had a crazy dream.

**36** One of the protesters told the reporter (that) war didn't solve any problems.

---

Long ago Wayne's parents told him:

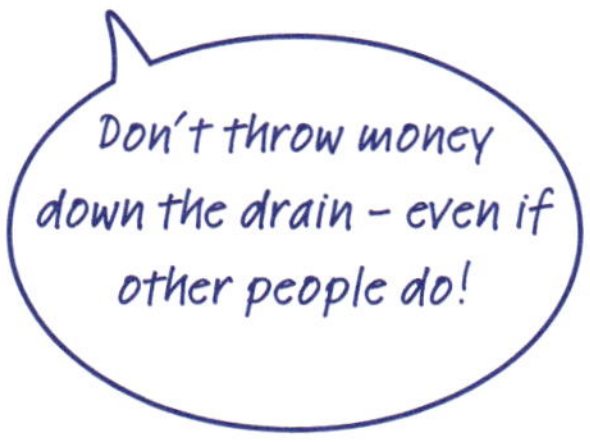

Long ago Wayne's parents told him *not to throw* money down the drain - even if other people did!

**Also correct:**
Long ago Wayne's parents told him *that he shouldn't throw* money down the drain - even if other people *did*!

to throw money down the drain – *Geld zum Fenster hinauswerfen*


Grammar Tandem Activities
ISBN: 978-3-12-581180-5

## 6 a Reported speech: Partner B (results)

**41** Mrs Mason asked her brother Elliot why he hadn't asked her for help.

**42** She wanted to know from her boss if / whether she had to work on Saturdays, too.

**43** The teacher asked if / whether everybody had done the exercises for that day.

**44** The young man asked how much the trainers in the shop window were.

**45** My friends wanted to know if / whether Germany had won the football match.

**46** The teacher asked his pupils if / whether they read any newspapers.

**51** Ron and Joe asked the girls who they were waiting for.

**52** All the pupils asked Mrs Hunt why she hadn't corrected their tests yet.

**53** After the job interview Jane wondered if / whether she would really get that job.

**54** Mrs McLean looked up to the sky and wondered if / whether it was going to rain.

**55** Mr Hilton wanted to know angrily why Simon couldn't stop talking.

**56** Lynn and Victoria asked the new boy what he had done the weekend before.

**61** Mrs Taylor told her children to wash their hands before they sat down.

(Mrs Taylor told her children that they should wash their hands before they sat down.)

**62** Doctor Brown advised his patients not to smoke, and to do more sport.

**63** Mr Clark ordered some boys not to kick the ball into his garden.

**64** Little Kitty asked her mother to give her an apple.

**65** The English teacher told some pupils not to be so lazy.

(The English teacher told some pupils that they shouldn't be so lazy.)

**66** Mrs Powell told her son to lay the table.

(Mrs Powell told her son that he should lay the table.)

Grandfather explained:

Grandfather explained *(that)* you *couldn't* turn the clocks back - no matter how hard you *tried*.

to turn the clocks back – *die Zeit zurückdrehen*

Grammar Tandem Activities
ISBN: 978-3-12-581180-5

## 6b Reported speech: Partner A (Questions and commands)

| | |
|---|---|
| 11 | The ambulance man asked the drivers: "Are you feeling all right?" |
| 12 | The policewoman told Jerry: "Show me your driving licence, please." |
| 13 | The teacher asked: "What part of the text can't you understand, Daniel?" |
| 14 | Our neighbours asked us: "Did you hear about the terrible accident?" |
| 15 | Sue asked her friend Cathy: "Wait for me in front of the disco." |
| 16 | The police wondered: "Who are the thieves who stole the money?" |
| 21 | Rosanna wondered: "Can I really earn enough money for that journey?" |
| 22 | She asked him: "Won't you have another piece of cake?" |
| 23 | The teacher wanted to know: "Have you finished the exercises yet, Alex?" |
| 24 | Mrs Croft told her husband: "Don't forget to buy tickets for the concert." |
| 25 | Sally asked her guests: "Do you prefer tea or coffee?" |
| 26 | A sign informed the tourists: "Don't throw anything out of the window." |
| 31 | They advised their kids: "Don't spend all your pocket money on sweets." |
| 32 | Another tourist asked us: "Which of the museums have you visited?" |
| 33 | The store detective asked the young man: "What are you doing here?" |
| 34 | An old lady wanted to know: "Does the next train to York leave at 12.41?" |
| 35 | The children asked their grandmother: "Tell us an exciting story, please." |
| 36 | The quiz show host wanted to know: "Who were the first astronauts who walked on the moon?" |

## 6b Reported speech: Partner B (Statements)

| | |
|---|---|
| 41 | The farmers complained: „It hasn't rained for more than a month." |
| 42 | Peter promised Susan: „I will write you a letter if you give me your address." |
| 43 | Harry told his parents: „I was surprised that I didn't make more mistakes." |
| 44 | Kelly explained: „When I go out with friends, I usually wear blue jeans." |
| 45 | Robin told Doctor Atkins: „My arm is still hurting a little." |
| 46 | The advert said: „We are looking for a friendly person who speaks English." |
| 51 | Father went to bed and said: „I have to get up very early tomorrow." |
| 52 | The young man explained: „We noticed the danger too late." |
| 53 | Neil told his girlfriend: „Other girls don't mean anything to me." |
| 54 | Tanya said: „I didn't know anything because I hadn't expected a test." |
| 55 | Grandfather remarked: „Last week I felt terrible because I had a bad cold." |
| 56 | Cindy told her boyfriend: „I have found your keys in my car." |
| 61 | Mrs Wilson added: „Last year we didn't go on holiday to Italy." |
| 62 | The man in uniform said: „The train to Sheffield doesn't leave until 11.17." |
| 63 | The teacher went on: „I want to know who has made such a mess." |
| 64 | Mr King told the parents: „Your daughter isn't doing well at school." |
| 65 | She went on angrily: „You won't see me again, Richard." |
| 66 | Mrs Adams told her son: „You can't play football before you have done your homework." |


Grammar Tandem Activities
ISBN: 978-3-12-581180-5

Klett

## 6 b Reported speech: Partner A (results)

11 The ambulance man asked the drivers if / whether they were feeling all right.

12 The policewoman told Jerry to show her his driving licence.

13 The teacher asked Daniel what part of the text he couldn't understand.

14 Our neighbours asked us if / whether we had heard about the terrible accident.

15 Sue asked her friend Cathy to wait for her in front of the disco.

16 The police wondered who the thieves were who had stolen the money.

21 Rosanna wondered if / whether she could really earn enough money for that journey.

22 She asked him if / whether he wouldn't have another piece of cake.

23 The teacher wanted to know if / whether Alex had finished the exercises yet.

24 Mrs Croft told her husband not to forget to buy tickets for the concert.
(Mrs Croft told her husband that he shouldn't forget to buy tickets for the concert.)

25 Sally asked her guests if / whether they preferred tea or coffee.

26 A sign informed the tourists not to throw anything out of the window.
(A sign informed the tourists that they shouldn't throw anything out of the window.)

31 They advised their kids not to spend all their pocket money on sweets.

32 Another tourist asked us which of the museums we had visited.

33 The store detective asked the young man what he was doing there.

34 An old lady wanted to know if / whether the next train to York left at 12.41.

35 The children asked their grandmother to tell them an exciting story.

36 The quiz show host wanted to know who the first astronauts had been who had walked on the moon.

---

Somebody added:

*Lovers have always seen life through rose-coloured glasses, but when it is over they often paint a black picture of everything.*

Somebody added *(that)* lovers *had* always *seen* life through rose-coloured glasses, but when it *was* over they often *painted* a black picture of everything.

to see sthg. through rose-coloured glasses – *etw. durch eine rosarote Brille sehen*
to paint a black picture – *ein düsteres Bild malen, schwarz sehen*

Grammar Tandem Activities
ISBN: 978-3-12-581180-5

## 6 b Reported speech: Partner B (results)

**41** The farmers complained (that) it hadn't rained for more than a month.

**42** Peter promised Susan (that) he would write her a letter if she gave him her address.

**43** Harry told his parents (that) he had been surprised that he hadn't made more mistakes.

**44** Kelly explained (that) when she went out with friends, she usually wore blue jeans.

**45** Robin told Doctor Atkins (that) his arm was still hurting a little.

**46** The advert said (that) they were looking for a friendly person who spoke English.

**51** Father went to bed and said (that) he had to get up very early the next / following day.

**52** The young man explained (that) they had noticed the danger too late.

**53** Neil told his girlfriend (that) other girls didn't mean anything to him.

**54** Tanya said (that) she hadn't known anything because she hadn't expected a test.

**55** Grandfather remarked (that) the week before he had felt terrible because he had had a bad cold.

**56** Cindy told her boyfriend (that) she had found his keys in her car.

**61** Mrs Wilson added (that) the year before they hadn't gone on holiday to Italy.

**62** The man in uniform said (that) the train to Sheffield didn't leave until 11.17.

**63** The teacher went on (that) he / she wanted to know who had made such a mess.

**64** Mr King told the parents (that) their daughter wasn't doing well at school.

**65** She went on angrily that Richard wouldn't see her again.

**66** Mrs Adams told her son (that) he couldn't play football before he had done his homework.

---

Mrs Newman, the head teacher, asked Mr Jones:

Mrs Newman, the head teacher, asked Mr Jones *why he didn't send* those boys to *her* if they *tried* to walk all over *him* in *his* Maths lessons.

to walk all over somebody – *jdm. auf der Nase herumtanzen*


Grammar Tandem Activities
ISBN: 978-3-12-581180-5

## 6c Reported speech: Partner A (Statements, questions, commands)

| | |
|---|---|
| 11 | The doctor asked Mr Howard: "When will you give up smoking?" |
| 12 | The shop assistant advised me: "Try on another size." |
| 13 | Six-year-old Kevin shouted: "I often ride my bike, but I never fall off." |
| 14 | The hotel manager asked us: "Did you enjoy your sightseeing trip?" |
| 15 | Mike told his girlfriend: "Phone me this afternoon." |
| 16 | Lara said: "I walked home from town after I missed the last bus." |
| 21 | The mountain guide told us: "I'm sure you will like the Swiss mountains." |
| 22 | Mother asked me: "Why has nobody told me about the problems?" |
| 23 | The teacher ordered Paula Pinter: "Don't do your homework at school!" |
| 24 | Julie told her friend: "When the lake has frozen, we can go ice-skating." |
| 25 | Mum told me: "Clean your teeth before you go to bed." |
| 26 | At last the teacher wanted to know: "Does anybody know the answer?" |
| 31 | Mrs Stevenson told little Jim: "Don't hit other children." |
| 32 | Uncle Ike said: "The beach was so crowded that we didn't go swimming." |
| 33 | All the pupils wondered: "Why can't we do the test tomorrow?" |
| 34 | Most people answered: "We do sport because it keeps us fit." |
| 35 | I asked him: "Where did you spend your holiday last year?" |
| 36 | Gina told her boyfriend: "Don't kiss me when my parents are watching us." |

## 6c Reported speech: Partner B (Statements, questions, commands)

| | |
|---|---|
| 41 | Dad advised me: „Don't ride your bike without a helmet!" |
| 42 | Amy asked me with a look of surprise: „Didn't you get an invitation?" |
| 43 | Linda told Simon: „I waited for you till half past eight." |
| 44 | My friend Alan wanted to know: „Will I get a postcard from you?" |
| 45 | Ellen told Claire: „Phone me as soon as you have done your homework." |
| 46 | The doctor told Mr Cook: „You won't get well again without an operation." |
| 51 | Mrs Campbell wondered: „Why doesn't my husband phone me?" |
| 52 | A journalist said: „I can't understand why terrorists do things like that." |
| 53 | Mrs Wilder remarked: „I don't think the guests have arrived yet." |
| 54 | The TV reporter asked the coach: „Why did the team lose this match?" |
| 55 | Mother advised me: „Ask somebody for help if you don't know what to do." |
| 56 | A sign told the park visitors: „Don't play any ball games here." |
| 61 | The old man explained: „I didn't see that the car in front of me had stopped." |
| 62 | Mrs Spencer advised her daughter: „Don't forget what I told you." |
| 63 | The passengers wanted to know: „Does this train stop at Shoreham?" |
| 64 | A fireman reported: „We are getting the fire under control." |
| 65 | The old lady told the waitress: „Bring me another cup of tea, please." |
| 66 | In the job interview the boss asked Mr Young: „How long have you been unemployed?" |


ISBN: 978-3-12-581180-5

## 6c Reported speech: Partner A (results)

**11** The doctor asked Mr Howard when he would give up smoking.

**12** The shop assistant advised me to try on another size.

**13** Six-year-old Kevin shouted (that) he often rode his bike, but (that) he never fell off.

**14** The hotel manager asked us if / whether we had enjoyed our sightseeing trip.

**15** Mike told his girlfriend to phone him that afternoon.

(Mike told his girlfriend that she should phone him that afternoon.)

**16** Lara said (that) she had walked home from town after she had missed the last bus.

**21** The mountain guide told us (that) he / she was sure (that) we would like the Swiss mountains.

**22** Mother asked me why nobody had told her about the problems.

**23** The teacher ordered Paula Pinter not to do her homework at school.

**24** Julie told her friend (that) when the lake had frozen, they could go ice-skating.

**25** Mum told me to clean my teeth before I went to bed.

(Mum told me that I should clean my teeth before I went to bed.)

**26** At last the teacher wanted to know if / whether anybody knew the answer.

**31** Mrs Stevenson told little Jim not to hit other children.

(Mrs Stevenson told little Jim that he shouldn't hit other children.)

**32** Uncle Ike said (that) the beach had been so crowded that they hadn't gone swimming.

**33** All the pupils wondered why they couldn't do the test the next / following day.

**34** Most people answered (that) they did sport because it kept them fit.

**35** I asked him where he had spent his holiday the year before.

**36** Gina told her boyfriend not to kiss her when her parents were watching them.

(Gina told her boyfriend that he shouldn't kiss her when her parents were watching them.)

---

Alice told her friend Karen:

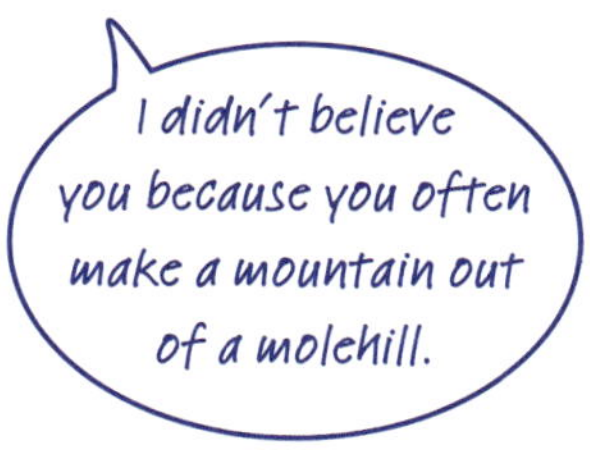

Alice told her friend Karen *(that) she hadn't believed her* because *she* often *made* a mountain out of a molehill.

to make a mountain out of a molehill – *aus einer Mücke einen Elefanten machen*


Grammar Tandem Activities
ISBN: 978-3-12-581180-5

## 6c Reported speech: Partner B (results)

41 Dad advised me not to ride my bike without a helmet.

42 Amy asked me with a look of surprise if / whether I / we hadn't got an invitation.

43 Linda told Simon (that) she had waited for him till half past eight.

44 My friend Alan wanted to know if / whether he would get a postcard from me / us.

45 Ellen told Claire to phone her as soon as she had done her homework.

(Ellen told Claire that she should phone her as soon as she had done her homework.)

46 The doctor told Mr Cook (that) he wouldn't get well again without an operation.

51 Mrs Campbell wondered why her husband didn't phone her.

52 A journalist said (that) he / she couldn't understand why terrorists did things like that.

53 Mrs Wilder remarked (that) she didn't think the guests had arrived yet.

54 The TV reporter asked the coach why the team had lost that match.

55 Mother advised me to ask somebody for help if I / we didn't know what to do.

56 A sign told the park visitors not to play any ball games there.

(A sign told the park visitors that they shouldn't play any ball games there.)

61 The old man explained (that) he hadn't seen that the car in front of him had stopped.

62 Mrs Spencer advised her daughter not to forget what she had told her.

63 The passengers wanted to know if / whether that train stopped at Shoreham.

64 A fireman reported (that) they were getting the fire under control.

65 The old lady told the waitress to bring her another cup of tea.

(The old lady told the waitress that she should bring her another cup of tea.)

66 In the job interview the boss asked Mr Young how long he had been unemployed.

---

Jason asked his favourite football star:

Does a professional footballer practise even when it is raining cats and dogs?

Jason asked his favourite football star *if / whether* a professional footballer *practised* even when it *was raining* cats and dogs.

to rain cats and dogs – *wie aus Kübeln gießen, wie aus Eimern schütten*

Grammar Tandem Activities
ISBN: 978-3-12-581180-5

# 7 Grammar mix

## Information for the teacher

### 1. Inhalte:

Wie der Begriff *Grammar mix* schon sagt, handelt es sich um eine bunte Mischung aus fünf Grammatikthemen. Jedem Thema ist eine Farbe zugeordnet:

- blue: The 'to-infinitive' or (preposition +) 'gerund'?
- green: 'Some' or 'any'? (… and their compounds)
- red: Adjective' or 'adverb'?
- white: 'Each other' or '-self / -selves'?
- yellow: 'Much' or 'many'?

Hinter diesen Inhalten steht eine Vielfalt von Regeln. Deshalb sind die Hinweise dazu auf dem Blatt *7 Grammar mix: Instructions* anders als bisher sehr kurz gehalten. Die Arbeit mit dem Material setzt voraus, dass diese Regeln noch vage bekannt sind. So dient das Üben dazu, ein (Sprach-)Gefühl für deren korrekte Anwendung zu entwickeln.

### 2. Spielversionen:

*Grammar mix* ist ein „Fußball-Lernspiel", das so aufgebaut ist, dass *zwei Spielversionen* möglich sind – und das in doppelter Hinsicht. Zum einen können die *16 tasks* bzw. *results* einer jeden Farbe so kopiert werden, dass *Spielkärtchen* entstehen mit einer Aufgabe auf der Vorderseite und deren Lösung auf der Rückseite. **(Kärtchenversion)**

Zum andern können die DIN-A4 Seiten mit den Aufgaben und Lösungen entlang der punktierten Linie in der Mitte in *zwei Hälften* geteilt werden, so dass in jeder Farbe *zwei DIN-A5 Aufgaben- bzw. Lösungsblöcke mit je 8 tasks bzw. results* entstehen – ein Block für Spieler A und einer für Spieler B. Spieler A bearbeitet dann von jeder Farbe die *tasks 1–8* und hat die *results 9–16* auf seiner Rückseite. Bei Spieler B verhält es sich umgekehrt, so dass sich beide *gegenseitig korrigieren* können. **(Blockversion)**

Die Blockversion erspart Ihnen das aufwendige Zuschneiden, Aufbewahren und Überprüfen der 80 Kärtchen auf deren Vollständigkeit. Statt jeweils das oberste Kärtchen vom Stapel der gewürfelten Farbe zu bearbeiten, würfeln die Spieler bei der *Blockversion* neben der Farbe mit einem Zahlenwürfel (1–6 Augen) eine Zahl. Sie rücken mit ihrer Spielfigur *auf ihrer Zahlenreihe entlang des Fußballfeldes*, auf dem sie spielen, um die gewürfelte Augenzahl vor. Dann bearbeiten sie die gewürfelte Aufgabe aus ihrem Aufgabenblock. Da *Spieler A* stets die *Aufgaben 1–8* zu lösen hat, findet man innerhalb seiner Zahlenreihe auch nur diese Zahlen. Bei *Spieler B* handelt es sich um die *Aufgaben bzw. Zahlen 9–16*. Aus diesem Grund sollten beide Spieler zu gegebener Zeit ihre „Rollen" und damit ihre *Aufgabenblöcke tauschen*. (Für die Kärtchenversion sind die Zahlenreihen entlang des Spielfeldes ohne Bedeutung.)

Neben der Kärtchen- bzw. Blockversion stehen zwei Spielfelder zur Auswahl: *Football-amateurs* und *Football-professionals*. Die Aufgaben und damit der *Schwierigkeitsgrad* sind gleich, allein die Spielregeln unterscheiden sich.

Bei der Version für *amateurs* geht es einfach entlang der punktierten Linien hin und her – von Ball zu Ball, bis ein Tor erzielt wird. Wie das viel komplexere Spielfeld *Football-professionals* erahnen lässt, hat der Gegenspieler durch *taktisches Bewegen seines Torhüters und Verteidigers* die Möglichkeit mit Geschick (und Glück, wie die Spielregeln zeigen) ein Tor zu verhindern. Näheres zu dieser Spielversion entnehmen Sie bitte dem Kapitel

*Spielverlauf* auf dem Blatt *7 Grammar mix: Instructions (for professionals).* Vieles spricht jedoch dafür am Anfang die Kombination aus *Blockversion* und Spielfeld *Football-amateurs* zu wählen.

### 3. Fertigstellen des Spiels:

Bevor Sie das Spiel fertig stellen, sollten Sie sich entscheiden, welche Spielversion Sie wählen. Dann können Sie gezielt die Aufgaben / Lösungen kopieren, das Spielfeld vorbereiten und das Spielzubehör bereitstellen.

**a) Aufgaben / Lösungen:**
Haben Sie sich für die Blockversion entschieden, so kopieren Sie die *tasks* und *results* nicht als Vorder- und Rückseite auf dasselbe Blatt, sondern Sie benutzen zwei verschiedene Blätter in den Farben, die oben auf den Kopiervorlagen angegeben sind.

Sowohl die *tasks* als auch die *results* teilen Sie entlang der punktierten Linie in der Mitte in zwei **DIN-A5 Hälften**: die eine für *Player A* und die andere für *Player B*. Danach stecken Sie für *Player A* jeweils die *tasks 1–8* und die *results 9–16* (= Lösungen des Gegenspielers) in eine DIN-A5 **Folienhülle** und schieben zur Verstärkung einen auf DIN-A5 zugeschnittenen Pappkarton dazwischen.
Bei *Player B* verhält es sich *umgekehrt*. So verfahren Sie bei allen 5 Farben.
Wenn Sie anschließend alle DIN-A5 Folienhüllen eines Spielers mit einem Heftstreifen zusammenheften, erhält jeder Spieler seine eigene fünfteilige „Aufgabensammlung“ (Abb. 1) mit den Lösungen des Gegenspielers auf den Rückseiten.

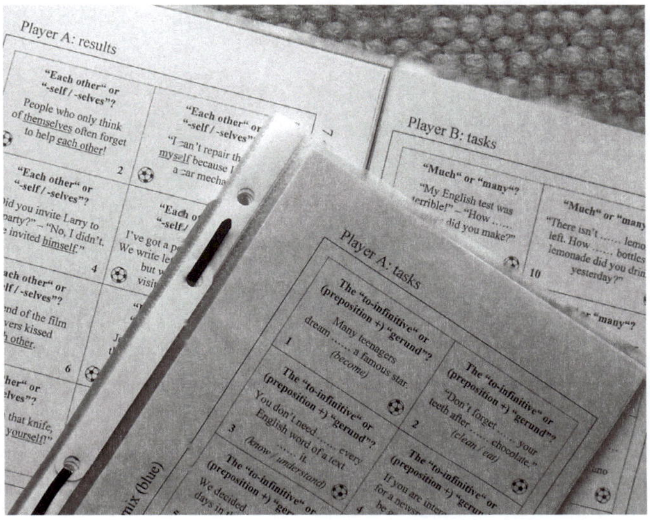

Abb. 1

Haben Sie die Kärtchenversion gewählt, so empfehle ich Ihnen folgendes Vorgehen beim *Erstellen von Kopiervorlagen* für die Kärtchen:

1. Fertigen Sie aus dem Kopiervorlagenheft *getrennte Kopien* von den Vorder- und Rückseiten der Kärtchen (*tasks* und *results*) an.
2. Schneiden Sie die beiden Blöcke aus jeweils 8 Kärtchen exakt *entlang der durchgezogenen Umrisslinie* aus.
3. Legen Sie die ausgeschnittenen Blöcke im *Hochformat* exakt in der linken oberen Ecke des Kopierfensters an. Vergrößern Sie die Blöcke mit dem **Reprofaktor 175 %** auf weißes Kopierpapier. Damit haben Sie *vergrößerte Kopiervorlagen*, deren Breite genau dem DIN-A4 Format entspricht und die Sie viel exakter im Kopierfenster anlegen können als ein Kopiervorlagenheft.

Mit diesen Kopiervorlagen können Sie die Vorder- und Rückseiten der Kärtchen viel leichter möglichst *deckungsgleich* übereinander kopieren. Machen Sie jetzt eine *Probekopie* mit Vorder- und Rückseite auf weißem Papier! Wie Sie dabei am besten vorgehen hängt vom jeweiligen Kopiergerät ab. Sollten die *punktierten Begrenzungslinien* der Kärtchen auf der Vorder- und Rückseite der Probekopie dennoch *zu wenig deckungsgleich* sein, so decken Sie diese auf der Rückseite der Kopiervorlage mit einem *Korrekturroller* ab. Beim späteren Zuschneiden der Kärtchen genügt es, wenn die punktierten Linien auf *einer* Seite vorhanden sind.

Zum eigentlichen Kopieren der Kärtchen verwenden Sie *farbiges Kopierpapier* gemäß den Vorgaben im Kopiervorlagenheft. Anschließend *folieren* Sie die *gesamten Seiten*, bevor Sie diese in Einzelkärtchen zerschneiden und die 80 Kärtchen *nach Farben sortiert* in einer *Kartenbox* aufbewahren.

**b) Spielfelder:**
Das Spielfeld *Football-amateurs* aus dem Kopiervorlagenheft ist in dieser Form einsatzbereit. Jedoch können die *Startfelder für Player A* und *Player B* vor den Zahlenreihen am unteren und oberen Spielfeldrand in den *beiden Farben der Spielfiguren* hervorgehoben werden.

Das Spielfeld *Football-professionals* **muss** farbig ausgestaltet werden. Wählen Sie jeweils eine *Mannschaftsfarbe* für *Team A* und *Team B* und malen Sie:

- sämtliche mit (A) bzw. (B) gekennzeichneten *Spielerpositionen* auf dem Spielfeld in diesen Farben aus – auch die beiden kleineren Kreise unterhalb bzw. oberhalb der Torhüter.
- Fahren Sie alle *Verbindungslinien* zwischen den Spielerpositionen innerhalb eines Teams in der *Mannschaftsfarbe* nach. (Beachten Sie, dass jedem Team eine eigene Linienstruktur zugeordnet ist und zwischen Torhüter und Verteidigung *keine* Verbindungslinie besteht.)
- Kolorieren Sie zum Schluss – wie schon beim Spielfeld *Football-amateurs* vorgeschlagen – die *Startfelder* für *Player A* und für *Player B* am unteren und oberen Spielfeldrand in den *Mannschaftsfarben*.

**c) Spielzubehör:**
Je nachdem, welche Spielversionen Sie miteinander kombinieren, benötigen Sie folgendes Spielzubehör:

| | **Blockversion** | **Kärtchenversion** |
|---|---|---|
| **Amateurs** | 1 Cent<br>je eine Figur in den Mannschaftsfarben | 1 cent |
| **Professionals** | 1 cent<br>je drei Figuren in den Mannschaftsfarben | 1 cent<br>je zwei Figuren in den Mannschaftsfarben |

# Instructions (for amateurs)

**Zum Arbeitsmaterial (Blockversion / Spielfeld *Football-amateurs*) gehören:**

1 Übungsanleitung *Instructions (for amateurs)*, 1 Spielfeld *Football-amateurs*, je ein DIN-A5 Aufgabenblatt in den Farben blau, grün, rot, weiß und gelb für *Player A (tasks 1–8)* und *Player B (tasks 9–16)*, je 1 Lösungsblatt DIN-A5 in denselben Farben für *Player A (results 9–16)* und *Player B (results 1–8)*, 1 Farbwürfel (blau, grün, rot, weiß, gelb, schwarz), 1 Würfel (1–6 Augen), 1 Ball (= 1 Cent), 2 Spielfiguren in verschiedenen Farben

## 1. Übungsgrundlage:

Da es sich bei diesem Spiel gleich um fünf verschiedene Grammatikinhalte handelt, müssen die Hinweise zu den Regeln sehr kurz und allgemein ausfallen:

| | |
|---|---|
| **zu blau:** | Regeln sind hier schwer zu fassen! Das *gerund* ist eine *-ing*-Form, die oft auf Begriffe mit Präpositionen folgt. Im Gegensatz dazu gibt es einige wichtige Verben, nach denen der *to-infinitive* stehen muss. |
| **zu grün:** | *Some* und seine Zusammensetzungen (compounds) benutzt man in *Aussagesätzen*. In *Fragen und verneinten Sätzen* steht fast immer *any*. Die Zusammensetzungen beziehen sich auf Dinge *(-thing)*, Personen *(-body)* oder Orte *(-where)*. |
| **zu rot:** | *Adjectives* beschreiben *Hauptwörter* näher, während sich *„-ly"-Adverbien* meistens auf *Verben* beziehen und die Art und Weise angeben, *wie* etwas getan wird. |
| **zu weiß:** | *Each other* zielt auf *Gegenseitigkeit* ab, *-self / -selves verweist zurück* auf die betreffende(n) Person(en) *selbst*. |
| **zu gelb:** | Kann man etwas *wirklich zählen*, so benutzt man *many*. Ist etwas *unzählbar*, so verwendet man *much*. Vorsicht! *Zeit* ist nicht zählbar, wohl aber die Minuten, Stunden, Tage. Bei einigen anderen abstrakten Begriffen ist das ähnlich! |

## 2. Spielvorbereitung:

Die beiden Spieler sitzen einander gegenüber und legen das Spielfeld *Football-amateurs* vor sich in der Tischmitte aus. *Player A* hat seine 5 Aufgabenblätter bzw. geheftete Aufgabensammlung mit den *tasks 1–8* in den Farben blau, grün, rot, weiß und gelb zur Hand, *Player B* ebenso, jedoch die *tasks 9–16*. Die Spieler legen den Ball (= 1 Cent) auf den Anstoßpunkt im Mittelkreis und stellen ihre Spielfigur auf das Startfeld für *Player A* bzw. *Player B* am Rand des Spielfeldes. Ein Farb- und ein Zahlenwürfel liegen bereit. Nun legen die Spieler noch fest, wer mit dem Würfeln beginnt.

Grammar Tandem Activities
ISBN: 978-3-12-581180-5

### 3. Spielverlauf:

Der Spieler, der an der Reihe ist, würfelt zuerst mit dem *Zahlenwürfel* eine Zahl. Er rückt mit seiner Spielfigur auf *seiner Zahlenreihe entlang des Spielfeldes* um die gewürfelte Augenzahl vor. Würfelt *Player A* beispielsweise eine Fünf, so landet er in seiner Zahlenreihe auf einem *Feld mit der Zahl 1*. Zeigt der *Farbwürfel* anschließend *gelb* an, so muss der Spieler vom *gelben Achterblock task 1* lösen. *Player B* überprüft die Lösung mit Hilfe der *results* auf der Rückseite seines gelben Achterblocks.

Beachte also - die gewürfelte Zahl gibt *nicht* die Nummer der zu bearbeitenden Aufgabe an, sondern bestimmt das Vorrücken mit der Spielfigur auf der Zahlenreihe. Hat sie das Ende der Reihe erreicht, kehrt sie wieder an den Anfang zurück.

War die **Antwort richtig**, so darf der Ball *um eine Station* weitergespielt werden. Das bedeutet entweder

- entlang der Verbindungslinie zwischen zwei Fußbällen,
- oder vom letzten Fußball ins gegnerische Tor,
- oder *nach einem Tor* vom Anstoßpunkt *nach vorne* zum nächsten Fußball.

Nach einer richtigen Antwort würfelt der Spieler eine weitere Aufgabe und versucht sie zu lösen. Dies setzt sich so lange fort, bis er einen *Fehler* macht - oder ein *Tor* erzielt. Dann wechselt der Ballbesitz.

War die **Antwort falsch**, so bleibt der Ball in seiner Position liegen und der *Gegner ist am Zug*.

Würfelt ein Spieler die **Farbe schwarz**, so entspricht das einem Fehlpass. Der Spieler muss zwar *um die gewürfelte Zahl vorrücken*, doch der Gegner ist nun am Ball und hat die Chance ein Tor zu erzielen. Der *Anstoß* nach einem Tor erfolgt immer vom *Mittelkreis* aus.

Ist ein Spiel mit *zwei Halbzeiten* geplant, so ist es ratsam für die zweite Spielhälfte die *Aufgabenblöcke (tasks) zu tauschen*.

Viel Spaß und Erfolg beim Spielen!


Grammar Tandem Activities
ISBN: 978-3-12-581180-5

# 7 Grammar mix: Football (amateurs)

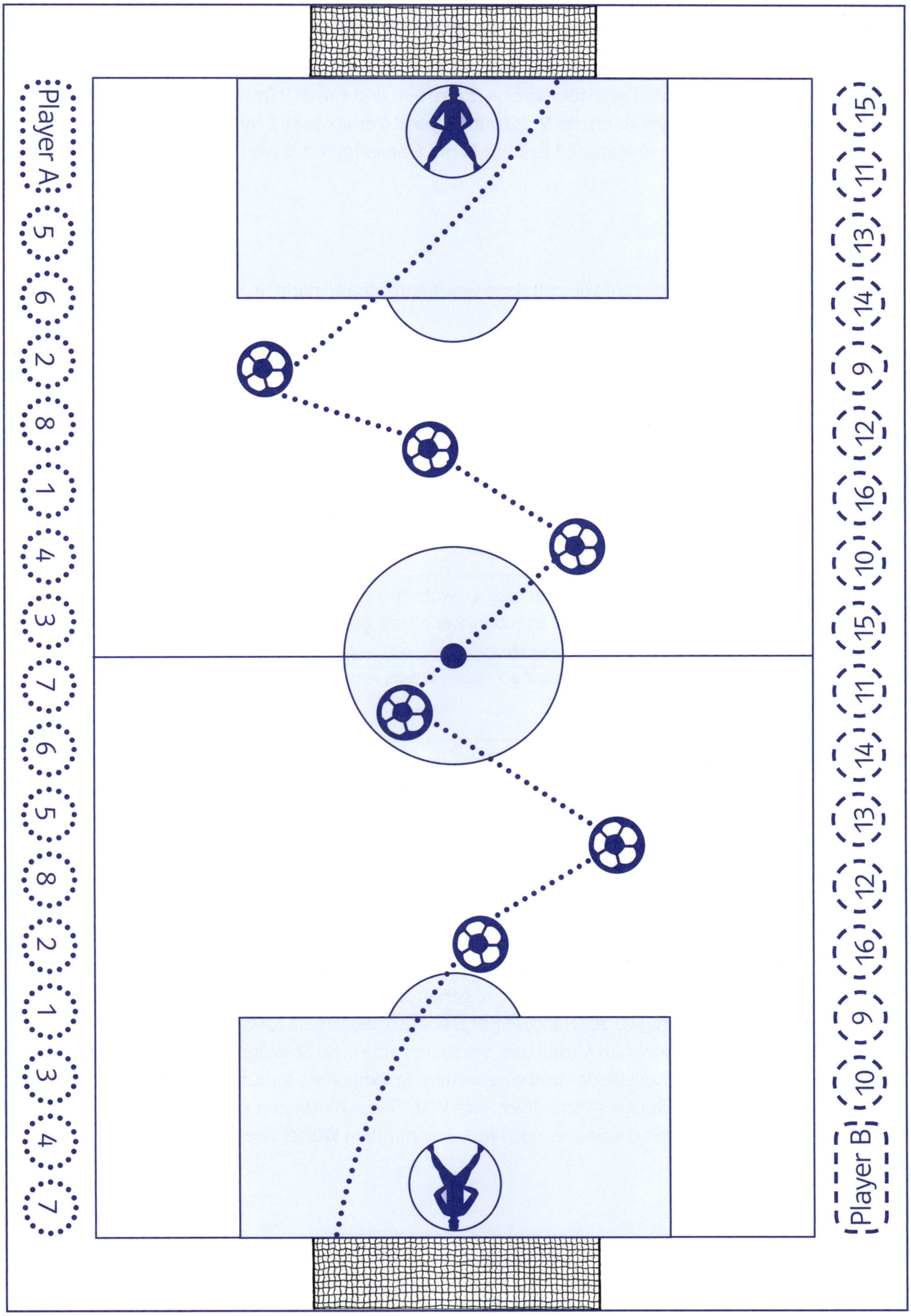



ISBN: 978-3-12-581180-5

## Grammar mix: Instructions (for professionals)

### Zum Arbeitsmaterial (Blockversion / Spielfeld *Football-professionals*) gehören:

1 Übungsanleitung *Instructions (for professionals)*, 1 Spielfeld *Football-professionals*, je ein DIN-A5 Aufgabenblatt in den Farben blau, grün, rot, weiß und gelb für *Player A (tasks 1–8)* und *Player B (tasks 9–16)*, je 1 Lösungsblatt DIN-A5 in denselben Farben für *Player A (results 9–16)* und *Player B (results 1–8)*, 1 Farbwürfel (blau, grün, rot, weiß, gelb, schwarz), 1 Würfel (1–6 Augen), 1 Ball (= 1 Cent), 6 Spielfiguren, davon jeweils 3 in denselben (Mannschafts-)Farben

### 1. Übungsgrundlage:

Da es sich bei diesem Spiel gleich um fünf verschiedene Grammatikinhalte handelt, müssen die Hinweise zu den Regeln sehr kurz und allgemein ausfallen:

| | |
|---|---|
| **zu blau:** | Regeln sind hier schwer zu fassen! Das *gerund* ist eine *-ing*-Form, die oft auf Begriffe mit Präpositionen folgt. Im Gegensatz dazu gibt es einige wichtige Verben, nach denen der *to-infinitive* stehen muss. |
| **zu grün:** | *Some* und seine Zusammensetzungen (compounds) benutzt man in *Aussagesätzen*. In *Fragen und verneinten Sätzen* steht fast immer *any*. Die Zusammensetzungen beziehen sich auf Dinge *(-thing)*, Personen *(-body)* oder Orte *(-where)*. |
| **zu rot:** | *Adjectives* beschreiben *Hauptwörter* näher, während sich *„-ly"-Adverbien* meistens auf *Verben* beziehen und die Art und Weise angeben, *wie* etwas getan wird. |
| **zu weiß:** | *Each other* zielt auf *Gegenseitigkeit* ab, *-self / -selves verweist zurück* auf die betreffende(n) Person(en) *selbst*. |
| **zu gelb:** | Kann man etwas *wirklich zählen*, so benutzt man *many*. Ist etwas *unzählbar*, so verwendet man *much*. Vorsicht! *Zeit* ist nicht zählbar, wohl aber die Minuten, Stunden, Tage. Bei einigen anderen abstrakten Begriffen ist das ähnlich! |

### 2. Spielvorbereitung:

Die beiden Spieler sitzen einander gegenüber und legen das Spielfeld *Football-professionals* vor sich in der Tischmitte aus. *Player A* hat seine 5 Aufgabenblätter bzw. geheftete Aufgabensammlung mit den *tasks 1–8* in den Farben blau, grün, rot, weiß und gelb zur Hand, *Player B* ebenso, jedoch die *tasks 9–16*. Die Spieler legen den Ball (= 1 Cent) auf den Anstoßpunkt im Mittelkreis. Sie stellen eine ihrer Spielfiguren auf das Startfeld für *Player A* bzw. *Player B* am Rand des Spielfeldes und eine weitere Spielfigur als Torhüter in die Mitte ihres Tores. Dann postieren sie ihre letzte Spielfigur als Verteidiger nach Wahl in der hintersten Reihe. Ein Farb- und ein Zahlenwürfel liegen bereit. Nun legen die Spieler noch fest, wer mit dem Würfeln beginnt.


Grammar Tandem Activities
ISBN: 978-3-12-581180-5

### 3. Spielverlauf:

**a) Allgemeine Spielregeln:**

1. Zu jedem Team gehören 3 Spielfiguren derselben Farbe:
   - ein Torhüter, der in Richtung der beiden Pfeile bewegt werden darf,
   - ein *Verteidiger*, dessen Position frei gewählt werden darf,
   - *Player A* bzw. *Player B*, der nur zum Würfeln der Aufgaben entlang seiner Zahlenreihe am Spielfeldrand hin und her bewegt wird.
2. Der Ball darf nur *entlang der Linien in der Farbe des eigenen Teams* gespielt werden. Er bewegt sich *unabhängig von den Spielfiguren* auf dem Feld.
3. Werden die Spielfiguren (Torhüter und Verteidiger) klug postiert, so können sie *die Flugbahn des Balles blockieren* (Taktik). Dann kann kein Tor erzielt werden.
4. Würfelt ein Spieler die **Farbe schwarz**, so *bleibt er im Ballbesitz* und *rückt um die gewürfelte Zahl vor*, kann aber keine Aufgabe lösen und somit den Ball nicht spielen. Des einen Pech – des andern Glück: der Gegner darf, wenn er will, seinen *Torhüter oder Verteidiger* zu seinem Vorteil um *eine Position verschieben*.

**b) Würfeln der Aufgaben:**
Der Spieler, der an der Reihe ist, würfelt zuerst mit dem *Zahlenwürfel* eine Zahl. Er rückt mit seiner Spielfigur auf *seiner Zahlenreihe entlang des Spielfeldes* um die gewürfelte Augenzahl vor. Würfelt *Player A* beispielsweise eine Fünf, so landet er in seiner Zahlenreihe auf einem *Feld mit der Zahl 1*. Zeigt der *Farbwürfel* anschließend *gelb* an, so muss der Spieler vom *gelben Achterblock task 1* lösen. *Player B* überprüft die Lösung mit Hilfe der *results* auf der Rückseite seines gelben Achterblocks. Beachte also:

- Die gewürfelte Zahl gibt *nicht* die Nummer der zu bearbeitenden Aufgabe an, sondern bestimmt das Vorrücken mit der Spielfigur auf der Zahlenreihe. Hat sie das Ende der Reihe erreicht, kehrt sie wieder an den Anfang zurück.

**c) Richtige und falsche Lösungen:**
War die **Antwort richtig**, so darf der Ball *um eine Station* weitergespielt werden,

- beim Anstoß *nach vorne* zum nächsten Spieler,
- entlang der Verbindungslinie zwischen zwei Spielern,
- von einem Stürmer *ins gegnerische Tor*,
- oder eine eigene *Spielfigur* kann um *eine Position* verschoben werden.

War die **Antwort falsch**, dann *wechselt der Ball* zum *nächstgelegenen Spieler* des gegnerischen Teams *hinter der Position des Balles*, und der Gegner ist am Zug. Ein Team darf so lange den Ball spielen, bis ein *Fehler* gemacht – oder ein *Tor* erzielt wird. Der *Anstoß* nach einem Tor erfolgt immer vom *Mittelkreis* aus.
Ist ein Spiel mit *zwei Halbzeiten* geplant, so ist es ratsam für die zweite Spielhälfte *die Aufgabenblöcke (tasks) zu tauschen*.

Viel Spaß und Erfolg beim Spielen!

Grammar Tandem Activities
ISBN: 978-3-12-581180-5

# 7 Grammar mix: Football (professionals)

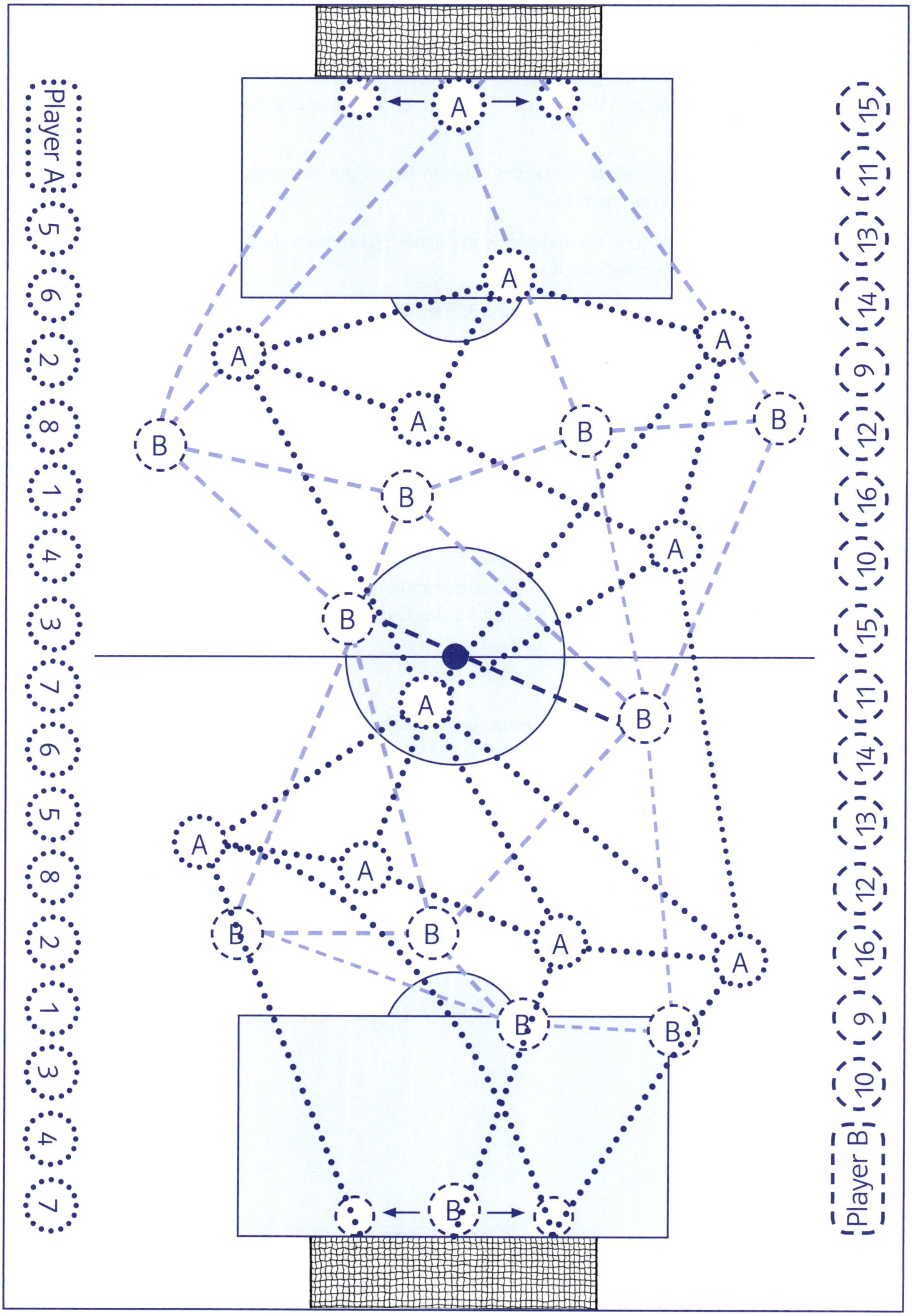



Grammar Tandem Activities
ISBN: 978-3-12-581180-5

## Grammar mix (blue), Player A: tasks

| | |
|---|---|
| **The 'to-infinitive' or (preposition +) gerund?**<br>Many teenagers dream … a famous star.<br>*(become)*<br>1 | **The 'to-infinitive' or (preposition +) gerund?**<br>"Don't forget … your teeth after … chocolate."<br>*(clean / eat)*<br>2 |
| **The 'to-infinitive' or (preposition +) gerund?**<br>You don't need … every English word of a text … it.<br>*(know / understand)*<br>3 | **The 'to-infinitive' or (preposition +) gerund?**<br>If you are interested … for a newspaper, you must be good … reports.<br>*(work / write)*<br>4 |
| **The 'to-infinitive' or (preposition +) gerund?**<br>We decided … our holidays in the Alps because we enjoy … .<br>*(spend / climb)*<br>5 | **The 'to-infinitive' or preposition +) gerund?**<br>Americans are famous … lots of barbecues.<br>*(have)*<br>6 |
| **The 'to-infinitive' or (preposition +) gerund?**<br>Simon's boss can't stand … late for work.<br>*(be)*<br>7 | **The 'to-infinitive' or (preposition +) gerund?**<br>The team is disappointed … the match, but it hopes … the next one.<br>*(lose / win)*<br>8 |

## Grammar mix (blue), Player B: tasks

| | |
|---|---|
| **The 'to-infinitive' or (preposition +) gerund?**<br>People who are over fifty often have only a small chance … a job again.<br>*(get)*<br>9 | **The 'to-infinitive' or (preposition +) gerund?**<br>If you want … healthy teeth, you should give … so many sweets.<br>*(have / eat)*<br>10 |
| **The 'to-infinitive' or (preposition +) gerund?**<br>"Please remember … me as soon as you have arrived."<br>*(phone)*<br>11 | **The 'to-infinitive' or (preposition +) gerund?**<br>Some pupils don't spend enough time … their home-work carefully.<br>*(do)*<br>12 |
| **The 'to-infinitive' or (preposition +) gerund?**<br>Although Simon promised … harder, he didn't even try … it.<br>*(work / do)*<br>13 | **The 'to-infinitive' or (preposition +) gerund?**<br>Many people say they can't imagine … without a mobile phone.<br>*(live)*<br>14 |
| **The 'to-infinitive' or (preposition +) gerund?**<br>If you are tired … a stupid programme, you should switch the TV off!<br>*(watch)*<br>15 | **The 'to-infinitive' or (preposition +) gerund?**<br>The Johnsons are looking forward … their relatives in Germany.<br>*(visit)*<br>16 |

Grammar Tandem Activities
ISBN: 978-3-12-581180-5

## Grammar mix (blue), Player B: results

| | |
|---|---|
| **The 'to-infinitive' or (preposition +) gerund?** If you want to have healthy teeth, you should give up eating so many sweets. 10 | **The 'to-infinitive' or (preposition +) gerund?** People who are over fifty often have only a small chance of getting a job again. 9 |
| **The 'to-infinitive' or (preposition +) gerund?** Some pupils don't spend enough time on doing their homework carefully. 12 | **The 'to-infinitive' or (preposition +) gerund?** "Please remember to phone me as soon as you have arrived." 11 |
| **The 'to-infinitive' or (preposition +) gerund?** Many people say they can't imagine living without a mobile phone. 14 | **The 'to-infinitive' or (preposition +) gerund?** Although Simon promised to work harder, he didn't even try to do it. 13 |
| **The 'to-infinitive' or (preposition +) gerund?** The Johnsons are looking forward to visiting their relatives in Germany. 16 | **The 'to-infinitive' or (preposition +) gerund?** If you are tired of watching a stupid programme, you should switch the TV off! 15 |

## Grammar mix (blue), Player A: results

| | |
|---|---|
| **The 'to-infinitive' or (preposition +) gerund?** "Don't forget to clean your teeth after eating chocolate." 2 | **The 'to-infinitive' or (preposition +) gerund?** Many teenagers dream of becoming a famous star. 1 |
| **The 'to-infinitive' or (preposition +) gerund?** If you are interested in working for a newspaper, you must be good at writing reports. 4 | **The 'to-infinitive' or (preposition +) gerund?** You don't need to know every English word of a text to understand it. 3 |
| **The 'to-infinitive' or (preposition +) gerund?** Americans are famous for having lots of barbecues. 6 | **The 'to-infinitive' or (preposition +) gerund?** We decided to spend our holidays in the Alps because we enjoy climbing. 5 |
| **The 'to-infinitive' or (preposition +) gerund?** The team is disappointed about losing the match, but it hopes to win the next one. 8 | **The 'to-infinitive' or (preposition +) gerund?** Simon's boss can't stand being late for work. 7 |


Grammar Tandem Activities
ISBN: 978-3-12-581180-5

## Grammar mix (green), Player A: tasks

| | |
|---|---|
| **'Some' or 'any'?**<br>**(<u>or</u>: -thing / -body / -where)**<br>"Listen, … must buy… cheese because there isn't … cheese left in the fridge."<br>1 | **'Some' or 'any'?**<br>**(<u>or</u>: -thing / -body / -where)**<br>Ron's vocabulary test was really terrible. He didn't know … .<br>2 |
| **'Some' or 'any'?**<br>**(<u>or</u>: -thing / -body / -where)**<br>Our dog Trixy ate all the sausages from the table because there wasn't … in the kitchen.<br>3 | **'Some' or 'any'?**<br>**(<u>or</u>: -thing / -body / -where)**<br>Frank was very unhappy with his birthday present because he got … to wear: a T-shirt.<br>4 |
| **'Some' or 'any'?**<br>**(<u>or</u>: -thing / -body / -where)**<br>Aunt Margaret didn't write … postcards because a one-week holiday is very short.<br>5 | **'Some' or 'any'?**<br>**(<u>or</u>: -thing / -body / -where)**<br>"My homework? I couldn't do … because I didn't find my workbook … ."<br>6 |
| **'Some' or 'any'?**<br>**(<u>or</u>: -thing / -body / -where)**<br>"Sorry, Dad, your car keys aren't … in your jacket."<br>7 | **'Some' or 'any'?**<br>**(<u>or</u>: -thing / -body / -where)**<br>"Let's look on a map. I think Hawaii is a group of islands … to the west of America."<br>8 |

## Grammar mix (green), Player B: tasks

| | |
|---|---|
| **'Some' or 'any'?**<br>**(<u>or</u>: -thing / -body / -where)**<br>"The new film at the cinema is really exciting. Has … seen it?"<br>9 | **'Some' or 'any'?**<br>**(<u>or</u>: -thing / -body / -where)**<br>"Do you have … afternoon lessons on Thursday?" – "Yes, we do."<br>10 |
| **'Some' or 'any'?**<br>**(<u>or</u>: -thing / -body / -where)**<br>"I'd like a bottle of milk and six eggs." – "… else, please?" – "No, that's all."<br>11 | **'Some' or 'any'?**<br>**(<u>or</u>: -thing / -body / -where)**<br>Yesterday … funny happened. We couldn't do our test. Our teacher had it … at home.<br>12 |
| **'Some' or 'any'?**<br>**(<u>or</u>: -thing / -body / -where)**<br>"I can't find my pencil case. Have you seen it … ?"<br>13 | **'Some' or 'any'?**<br>**(<u>or</u>: -thing / -body / -where)**<br>"Sally, there is … on the phone for you!"<br>14 |
| **'Some' or 'any'?**<br>**(<u>or</u>: -thing / -body / -where)**<br>There isn't … at our school on Saturdays because there aren't … lessons.<br>15 | **'Some' or 'any'?**<br>**(<u>or</u>: -thing / -body / -where)**<br>Every morning little Betty asks her grandma for … sweets.<br>16 |

Grammar Tandem Activities
ISBN: 978-3-12-581180-5

## Grammar mix (green), Player B: results

| | |
|---|---|
| **'Some' or 'any'?** **(or: -thing / -body / -where)** "Do you have any afternoon lessons on Thursday?" – "Yes, we do." ⚽ 10 | **'Some' or 'any'?** **(or: -thing / -body / -where)** "The new film at the cinema is really exciting. Has anybody seen it?" ⚽ 9 |
| **'Some' or 'any'?** **(or: -thing / -body / -where)** Yesterday something funny happened. We couldn't do our test. Our teacher had it some-where at home. ⚽ 12 | **'Some' or 'any'?** **(or: -thing / -body / -where)** "I'd like a bottle of milk and six eggs." – "Anything else, please?" – "No, that's all." ⚽ 11 |
| **'Some' or 'any'?** **(or: -thing / -body / -where)** "Sally, there is somebody on the phone for you!" ⚽ 14 | **'Some' or 'any'?** **(or: -thing / -body / -where)** "I can't find my pencil case. Have you seen it anywhere?" ⚽ 13 |
| **'Some' or 'any'?** **(or: -thing / -body / -where)** Every morning little Betty asks her grandma for some sweets. ⚽ 16 | **'Some' or 'any'?** **(or: -thing / -body / -where)** There isn't anybody at our school on Saturdays because there aren't any lessons. ⚽ 15 |

## Grammar mix (green), Player A: results

| | |
|---|---|
| **'Some' or 'any'?** **(or: -thing / -body / -where)** Ron's vocabulary test was really terrible. He didn't know anything. ⚽ 2 | **'Some' or 'any'?** **(or: -thing / -body / -where)** "Listen, somebody must buy some cheese because there isn't any cheese left in the fridge." ⚽ 1 |
| **Some' or 'any'?** **(or: -thing / -body / -where)** Frank was very unhappy with his birthday present because he got something to wear: a T-shirt. ⚽ 4 | **'Some' or 'any'?** **(or: -thing / -body / -where)** Our dog Trixy ate all the sausages from the table because there wasn't anybody in the kitchen. ⚽ 3 |
| **'Some' or 'any'?** **(or: -thing / -body / -where)** "My homework? I couldn't do any / anything because I didn't find my workbook anywhere." ⚽ 6 | **'Some' or 'any'?** **(or: -thing / -body / -where)** Aunt Margaret didn't write any postcards because a one-week holiday is very short. ⚽ 5 |
| **'Some' or 'any'?** **(or: -thing / -body / -where)** "Let's look on a map. I think Hawaii is a group of islands somewhere to the west of America." ⚽ 8 | **'Some' or 'any'?** **(or: -thing / -body / -where)** "Sorry, Dad, your car keys aren't anywhere in your jacket." ⚽ 7 |


Grammar Tandem Activities
ISBN: 978-3-12-581180-5

## Grammar mix (red), Player A: tasks

**Adjective or adverb?**
Mr Spencer felt … when he came home from hospital.
*(glad)*
1

**Adjective or adverb?**
Some fans waited … , others shouted … .
*(quiet / crazy)*
2

**Adjective or adverb?**
Mother said: "It's an … job. Come on, do it … !"
*(easy / quick)*
3

**Adjective or adverb?**
Do you think you will get … food at the fast food place?
*(healthy)*
4

**Adjective or adverb?**
Laura speaks English … , but her written tests aren't … .
*(good / good)*
5

**Adjective or adverb?**
When Sally saw her mark she smiled … .
*(happy)*
6

**Adjective or adverb?**
Some rock stars like to live … .
*(dangerous)*
7

**Adjective or adverb?**
Sometimes … pupils ask … questions.
*(stupid / clever)*
8

## Grammar mix (red), Player B: tasks

**Adjective or adverb?**
"Why don't you try it? It tastes … ."
*(good)*
9

**Adjective or adverb?**
Peter played … with his pen because some questions were very … .
*(nervous / difficult)*
10

**Adjective or adverb?**
It was an … match, but our team played quite … .
*(exciting / bad)*
11

**Adjective or adverb?**
"If you like to shop … , we can go to the department store over there."
*(cheap)*
12

**Adjective or adverb?**
"Be … ," the teacher said … .
*(quiet / angry)*
13

**Adjective or adverb?**
"Listen, my favourite song! Doesn't it sound … ?"
*(great)*
14

**Adjective or adverb?**
On rainy days drivers must drive … .
*(careful)*
15

**Adjective or adverb?**
If you write … , you won't make … mistakes.
*(slow / silly)*
16

Grammar Tandem Activities
ISBN: 978-3-12-581180-5

## Grammar mix (red), Player B: results

**Adjective or adverb?**
Peter played nervously with his pen because some questions were very difficult.
10

**Adjective or adverb?**
"Why don't you try it? It tastes good."
9

**Adjective or adverb?**
"If you like to shop cheaply, we can go to the department store over there."
12

**Adjective or adverb?**
It was an exciting match, but our team played quite badly.
11

**Adjective or adverb?**
"Listen, my favourite song! Doesn't it sound great?"
14

**Adjective or adverb?**
"Be quiet," the teacher said angrily.
13

**Adjective or adverb?**
If you write slowly, you won't make silly mistakes.
16

**Adjective or adverb?**
On rainy days drivers must drive carefully.
15

## Grammar mix (red), Player A: results

**Adjective or adverb?**
Some fans waited quietly, others shouted crazily.
2

**Adjective or adverb?**
Mr Spencer felt glad when he came home from hospital.
1

**Adjective or adverb?**
Do you think you will get healthy food at the fast food place?
4

**Adjective or adverb?**
Mother said: "It's an easy job. Come on, do it quickly."
3

**Adjective or adverb?**
When Sally saw her mark she smiled happily.
6

**Adjective or adverb?**
Laura speaks English well, but her written tests aren't good.
5

**Adjective or adverb?**
Sometimes stupid pupils ask clever questions.
8

**Adjective or adverb?**
Some rock stars like to live dangerously.
7


Grammar Tandem Activities
ISBN: 978-3-12-581180-5

## Grammar mix (white), Player A: tasks

**'Each other' or '-self / -selves'?**
"I can't repair the car … because I'm not a car mechanic."
1

**'Each other' or '-self / -selves'?**
People who only think of … often forget to help … !
2

**'Each other' or '-self / -selves'?**
I've got a penfriend in Italy. We write letters to … , but we have never visited … .
3

**'Each other' or '-self / -selves'?**
"Did you invite Larry to your party?" – "No, I didn't. He invited … ."
4

**'Each other' or '-self / -selves'?**
Jennifer was so angry that she locked … in her room.
5

**'Each other' or '-self / -selves'?**
At the end of the film the lovers kissed … .
6

**'Each other' or '-self / -selves'?**
We had to wash … in the cold river, but soon we liked it.
7

**'Each other' or '-self / -selves'?**
"Be careful with that knife, Linda. Don't cut … !"
8

## Grammar mix (white), Player B: tasks

**'Each other' or '-self / -selves'?**
Sometimes cats and dogs like … very much and even play with … .
9

**'Each other' or '-self / -selves'?**
Little Tom is crying because he has hurt … with a hammer.
10

**'Each other' or '-self / -selves'?**
Yesterday we watched a video of our football match. It was funny to see … playing.
11

**'Each other' or '-self / -selves'?**
Every morning a cat sits on our garden wall and cleans … .
12

**'Each other' or '-self / -selves'?**
Aunt Vicky is trying to teach … English with CDs.
13

**'Each other' or '-self / -selves'?**
Brothers and sisters often argue with … .
14

**'Each other' or '-self / -selves'?**
Isn't that funny? Lilian and Greg tried to phone … at exactly the same moment.
15

**'Each other' or '-self / -selves'?**
Little children find it funny to look at … in the mirror.
16

Grammar Tandem Activities
ISBN: 978-3-12-581180-5

## Grammar mix (white), Player B: results

**'Each other' or '-self / -selves'?**
Little Tom is crying because he has hurt himself with a hammer.
10

**'Each other' or '-self / -selves'?**
Sometimes cats and dogs like each other very much and even play with each other.
9

**'Each other' or '-self / -selves'?**
Every morning a cat sits on our garden wall and cleans itself.
12

**'Each other' or '-self / -selves'?**
Yesterday we watched a video of our football match. It was funny to see ourselves playing.
11

**'Each other' or '-self / -selves'?**
Brothers and sisters often argue with each other.
14

**'Each other' or '-self / -selves'?**
Aunt Vicky is trying to teach herself English with CDs.
13

**'Each other' or '-self / -selves'?**
Little children find it funny to look at themselves in the mirror.
16

**'Each other' or '-self / -selves'?**
Isn't that funny? Lilian and Greg tried to phone each other at exactly the same moment.
15

## Grammar mix (white), Player A: results

**'Each other' or '-self / -selves'?**
People who only think of themselves often forget to help each other!
2

**'Each other' or '-self / -selves'?**
"I can't repair the car myself because I'm not a car mechanic."
1

**'Each other' or '-self / -selves'?**
"Did you invite Larry to your party?" – "No, I didn't. He invited himself."
4

**'Each other' or '-self / -selves'?**
I've got a penfriend in Italy. We write letters to each other, but we have never visited each other.
3

**'Each other' or '-self / -selves'?**
At the end of the film the lovers kissed each other.
6

**'Each other' or '-self / -selves'?**
Jennifer was so angry that she locked herself in her room.
5

**'Each other' or '-self / -selves'?**
"Be careful with that knife, Linda. Don't cut yourself!"
8

**'Each other' or '-self / -selves'?**
We had to wash ourselves in the cold river, but soon we liked it.
7


Grammar Tandem Activities
ISBN: 978-3-12-581180-5

## Grammar mix (yellow), Player A: tasks

**'Much' or 'many'?**
Today … children eat too … chocolate and not enough fruit.
1

**'Much' or 'many'?**
"How … time did you need for that game?" – "Well, … hours. I didn't count them."
2

**'Much' or 'many'?**
Mrs Taylor wants to buy … books to read while she is on holiday.
3

**'Much' or 'many'?**
"Free time? I don't have … of it because my job is so stressful."
4

**'Much' or 'many'?**
… parents know that too … computer games are bad for their kids, but they buy them. Why?
5

**'Much' or 'many'?**
"Your skateboard is super, Tim, but it must have been very expensive. Tell me – how … was it?"
6

**'Much' or 'many'?**
"How … apples would you like, Mrs Beckham?"
7

**'Much' or 'many'?**
How … butter and how … eggs do you need for a cake?
8

## Grammar mix (yellow), Player B: tasks

**'Much' or 'many'?**
"My English test was terrible!" – "How … mistakes did you make?"
9

**'Much' or 'many'?**
"There isn't … lemonade left. How … bottles of lemonade did you drink yesterday?"
10

**'Much' or 'many'?**
I do so … sport because it's fun. But it's true that … sports cost money.
11

**'Much' or 'many'?**
"Don't take so … sugar, Kate! Hot chocolate is sweet enough without any sugar."
12

**'Much' or 'many'?**
Richard doesn't get … pocket money because he doesn't do … work at home. Is that okay?
13

**'Much' or 'many'?**
"My hobbies? I've got … of them, for example reading, playing the piano or taking photos."
14

**'Much' or 'many'?**
How … presents did Anne get for her birthday?
15

**'Much' or 'many'?**
… pupils think they get too … homework.
16

Grammar Tandem Activities
ISBN: 978-3-12-581180-5

## Grammar mix (yellow), Player B: results

| | |
|---|---|
| **'Much' or 'many'?**<br>"There isn't <u>much</u> lemonade left. How <u>many</u> bottles of lemonade did you drink yesterday?"<br>10 | **'Much' or 'many'?**<br>"My English test was terrible!" – "How <u>many</u> mistakes did you make?"<br>9 |
| **'Much' or 'many'?**<br>"Don't take so <u>much</u> sugar, Kate! Hot chocolate is sweet enough without any sugar."<br>12 | **'Much' or 'many'?**<br>I do so <u>much</u> sport because it's fun. But it's true that <u>many</u> sports cost money.<br>11 |
| **'Much' or 'many'?**<br>"My hobbies? I've got <u>many</u> of them, for example reading, playing the piano or taking photos."<br>14 | **'Much' or 'many'?**<br>Richard doesn't get <u>much</u> pocket money because he doesn't do <u>much</u> work at home. Is that okay?<br>13 |
| **'Much' or 'many'?**<br><u>Many</u> pupils think they get too <u>much</u> homework.<br>16 | **'Much' or 'many'?**<br>How <u>many</u> presents did Anne get for her birthday?<br>15 |

## Grammar mix (yellow), Player A: results

| | |
|---|---|
| **'Much' or 'many'?**<br>"How <u>much</u> time did you need for that game?" – "Well, <u>many</u> hours. I didn't count them."<br>2 | **'Much' or 'many'?**<br>Today <u>many</u> children eat too <u>much</u> chocolate and not enough fruit.<br>1 |
| **'Much' or 'many'?**<br>"Free time? I don't have <u>much</u> of it because my job is so stressful."<br>4 | **'Much' or 'many'?**<br>Mrs Taylor wants to buy <u>many</u> books to read while she is on holiday.<br>3 |
| **'Much' or 'many'?**<br>"Your skateboard is super, Tim, but it must have been very expensive. Tell me – how <u>much</u> was it?"<br>6 | **'Much' or 'many'?**<br><u>Many</u> parents know that too <u>many</u> computer games are bad for their kids, but they buy them. Why?<br>5 |
| **'Much' or 'many'?**<br>How <u>much</u> butter and how <u>many</u> eggs do you need for a cake?<br>8 | **'Much' or 'many'?**<br>"How <u>many</u> apples would you like, Mrs Beckham?"<br>7 |


Grammar Tandem Activities
ISBN: 978-3-12-581180-5

# 8 Mediation

## Instructions

### Zum Arbeitsmaterial gehören:

1 Übungsanleitung *Instructions*, je 1 Aufgabenblatt *8 Mediation* für Partner A und Partner B in einer der Versionen *Situation 1, 2, 3* oder *4*

### 1. Übungsgrundlage:

Der Sprachmittlungsteil *8 Mediation* steht in keinem direkten inhaltlichen Bezug zu den vorangehenden Grammatikthemen. Er nimmt jedoch das Prinzip der Partnerarbeit methodisch auf und wandelt das für Sprachmittlung übliche *Dreiergespräch* in einen *Dialog mit gegenseitiger Ergebniskontrolle* um.

In der typischen *Mediation-Situation* vermittelt gewöhnlich eine *dritte Person*, die sowohl Deutsch als auch Englisch spricht, zwischen einem *native speaker* (der nur Englisch spricht) und einer *weiteren Person*, die über keine oder nur unzureichende Englischkenntnisse verfügt. Deshalb muss zum einen vom Deutschen ins Englische und zum andern vom Englischen ins Deutsche übersetzt werden. Übersetzt bedeutet hier nicht wörtlich, wohl aber so, dass der Inhalt unverfälscht weitergegeben wird.

Soll ein *Dreiergespräch* in einen *Dialog* umgewandelt werden, so geht das nicht ohne Auswirkungen auf die *zu spielenden Rollen*:

- Die Person ohne Englischkenntnisse ist im Dialog nur noch eine *fiktive Person*, die nicht „real“ auftritt. Ihr Informationsbedarf, ihre Auskünfte, Wünsche und Bitten sind deshalb auf dem Aufgabenblatt *in Klammern gesetzt* und *kursiv gedruckt*. Sie prägen den Dialogverlauf jedoch entscheidend, da beide Gesprächspartner auf sie eingehen müssen.

- Im Rahmen der gegenseitigen Ergebniskontrolle muss auch der *native speaker*, der seiner Rolle nach nur Englisch spricht, die Fehler korrigieren, die der zweisprachige Partner beim Übersetzen ins Deutsche macht. Umgekehrt berichtigt dieser wiederum auch die Fehler im Englisch des *native speaker*. Diese paradoxe Situation ist jedoch die Kehrseite der gegenseitigen Ergebniskontrolle.

- Die als *Maßstab* für die gegenseitige Ergebniskontrolle vorgegebenen Lösungen sind *nicht die einzig richtigen*. Es gibt durchaus andere Möglichkeiten der sprachlichen Umsetzung, die jedoch nicht aufgeführt werden können.

Auf die Wortschatzangaben in Form von auf dem Kopf stehenden Fußnoten kann je nach Bedarf zurückgegriffen werden. Sie ermöglichen ein weitestgehend selbstständiges Arbeiten der Klasse.

### 2. Übungsziel:

Durch die Übung mit dem Arbeitsmaterial soll die Fähigkeit der Schüler gefördert werden, in der Fremdsprache auf wechselnde Gesprächssituationen flexibel und sprachlich angemessen reagieren zu können.

### 3. Übungsweise:

Der Dialog ist auf mündliche Partnerarbeit hin angelegt. Die beiden Partner sitzen einander gegenüber und machen sich zunächst mit dem *situativen Rahmen* und mit ihrer *Dialogrolle* vertraut. Dazu benötigt jeder sein eigenes Aufgabenblatt für Partner A bzw. Partner B, oder aber einer der beiden Partner hält das gemeinsame Blatt mit Vorder- und Rückseite so in der Hand, dass beide ihren Teil einsehen können.
Der Mund steht als Symbol für *Sprechen*, das Ohr als Symbol für *Zuhören* und *Fehler des Partners berichtigen*.

Es empfiehlt sich den Dialog so lange durchzuspielen, bis er möglichst fließend geführt werden kann, ohne die unten angegebene Vokabelliste gezielt zu Hilfe nehmen zu müssen. Darüber hinaus ist es durchaus sinnvoll, danach die Aufgabenblätter zu tauschen und die Rolle des Partners einzuüben.


Grammar Tandem Activities
ISBN: 978-3-12-581180-5

## Situation 1: Partner A

### At the restaurant

You are an *English-speaking tourist* from Germany. Your friend Tina doesn't speak any English. So you do the interpreting for her.

| **You, also for Tina (in English, of course!)** | **Listen to the waiter. Correct his mistakes.** | **You, to Tina (in German, of course!)** |
| --- | --- | --- |
| **Du:** Guten Tag. Könnten wir bitte die Speisekarte haben? | "Hello. Just a moment. / Wait a minute, please. – Here you are. What would you like to drink?" | **Du:** Er fragt, was … . |
| *(Tina: Ich hätte gerne ein Glas Orangensaft.)*<br><br>**Du:** Sie hätte gerne ein Glas Orangensaft und für mich bitte eine Flasche Mineralwasser. | "Thank you. Can I bring you something to eat?" | **Du:** Er … sich und will wissen, ob er … . |
| *(Tina: Frag ihn bitte, ob er das Steak auf der Speisekarte empfehlen kann.)*<br><br>**Du:** She asks if … . | "Yes. Lots of guests have it with chips and vegetables." | **Du:** Er sagt, dass … . |
| *(Tina: Ich mag kein Gemüse. Frag, ob ich statt Gemüse Salat haben kann.)*<br><br>**Du:** The steak on the menu for me, but she says that … . Can she … ? | "No problem. What would she prefer – lettuce or tomato salad?" | **Du:** Es ist … . Er will wissen, was … . |
| *(Tina: Eine Mischung von beiden Salaten wäre toll.)*<br><br>**Du:** She says that … . | "Okay, steak with chips and a mixed salad for her … ."<br><br>"And what about a dessert? We have fruit salad, different kinds / sorts of cake and ice cream." | **Du:** Es geht, Steak mit … .<br><br>Und er fragt, wie … . Sie haben … . |
| *(Tina: Ein Erdbeereis bitte.)*<br><br>**Du:** Erdbeereis für sie und ein Stück Apfelkuchen für mich bitte. | "Thank you very much for your order. The drinks will be ready in a minute." | **Du:** Er … sich für die … und sagt, dass … . |
| **Du:** Herr Ober, die Rechnung bitte. | "That's 16.25 altogether." | **Du:** Es … . |
| **Du:** Bitte sehr. Der Rest ist Trinkgeld. | "Thank you. Have a nice day." | **Du:** Er … sich und … . |

*Speisekarte* = menu, *Mineralwasser* = mineral water, *empfehlen* = (to) recommend, *grüner Salat* = lettuce,
*Mischung* = mixture, *die Rechnung* = the bill, *der Rest ist Trinkgeld* = keep the change

Grammar Tandem Activities
ISBN: 978-3-12-581180-5

## Situation 1: Partner B

### At the restaurant

You are an *English waiter* who serves the drinks and meals at an English restaurant. You are talking to an English-speaking guest from Germany, whose friend Tina does not speak any English.

| **Listen to your guest and correct his / her mistakes.** | **You, to your guests (in English, of course!)** | **Listen to your guest´s interpreting and correct his / her mistakes.** |
|---|---|---|
| "Hello. Could we have the menu, please?" | **Du:** Guten Tag. Einen Augenblick bitte. – Bitte sehr.<br>Was würden Sie gerne trinken? | „Er fragt, was wir gerne trinken würden." |
| "She would like a glass of orange juice and for me a bottle of mineral water, please." | **Du:** Danke schön. Darf ich Ihnen etwas zu essen servieren / bringen? | „Er bedankt sich und will wissen, ob er uns etwas zu essen servieren darf." |
| "She asks if you can recommend the steak on the menu." | **Du:** Ja, viele Gäste nehmen *(to have)* es mit Pommes frites und Gemüse. | „Er sagt, dass viele Gäste es mit Pommes frites und Gemüse nehmen." |
| "The steak on the menu for me, but she says that she doesn't like (any) vegetables. Can she have salad instead of vegetables?" | **Du:** Kein Problem. Was mag sie lieber – grünen Salat oder Tomatensalat? | „Es ist kein Problem. Er will wissen, was du lieber magst – grünen Salat oder Tomatensalat." |
| "She says that a mixture of both salads would be great." | **Du:** Okay, Steak mit Pommes frites und einem gemischten Salat für sie … .<br><br>Und wie wär's mit einem Nachtisch? Wir haben Obstsalat, verschiedene Sorten Kuchen und Eis. | „Es geht, Steak mit Pommes frites und einem gemischten Salat für dich … ."<br><br>„Und er fragt, wie es mit einem Nachtisch wäre. Sie haben Obstsalat, verschiedene Sorten Kuchen und Eis." |
| "Strawberry ice cream for her, and a piece of apple pie / apple cake for me, please." | **Du:** Vielen Dank für Ihre Bestellung. Die Getränke kommen sofort. | „Er bedankt sich für die Bestellung und sagt, dass die Getränke sofort kommen." |
| "Waiter, the bill please." | **Du:** Das macht 16,25 Pfund zusammen. | „Es macht / kostet zusammen 16,25 Pfund." |
| "Here you are. Keep the change." | **Du:** Danke schön. Einen schönen Tag noch. | „Er bedankt sich und wünscht uns noch einen schönen Tag." |

*servieren = (to) bring, lieber mögen = (to) prefer, grüner Salat = lettuce, gemischter Salat = mixed salad,*
*Nachtisch = dessert, Bestellung = order, die Getränke kommen sofort = the drinks will be ready in a minute*


Grammar Tandem Activities
ISBN: 978-3-12-581180-5

## Situation 2: Partner A

### At the hotel reception

Your grandparents have won a four-day journey to London. As your grandpa isn't fit enough to travel, your *grandma has asked you to go with her*. You agree, of course, but soon you find out that you have to do all the interpreting for her – like here at the reception of your *London hotel*.

| **You, also for your grandma (in English, of course!)** | **Listen to the hotel receptionist. Correct her mistakes.** | **You, to your grandma (in German, of course!)** |
|---|---|---|
| **Du:** Guten Morgen. Darf ich Ihnen ein paar Fragen stellen? | "Yes, of course. What's your problem?" | **Du:** Sie fragt, was … . |
| **Du:** Wir würden morgen gerne auf Besichtigungstour gehen. Würden Sie mit dem Bus oder mit der U-Bahn fahren? | "By bus. There are special sight-seeing buses. I can phone a bus company and book two seats for you." | **Du:** Sie würde … . Es gibt … . Sie kann … . |
| *(Oma: Frag bitte, ob es Besichtigungstouren mit deutsch-sprachigen Reiseführern gibt.)*<br><br>**Du:** Are there … ? | "Of course. Not all German tourists speak English perfectly." | **Du:** Selbstverständlich, denn nicht … . |
| *(Oma: Sie soll eine Fahrt für morgen Vormittag buchen. Und frag, was wir heute Nachmittag machen können.)*<br><br>**Du:** OK, please … . She also asks what … . | "Oh, the weather is great / fine. Why don't you visit the 'London Eye'. It isn't far from here." | **Du:** Sie meint, dass das … und fragt, warum … . Es ist … . |
| **Du:** Das ist eine gute Idee, aber ich bin mir sicher, dass es Oma schlecht werden wird, wenn wir damit fahren. | "I don't think so, because the 'London Eye' moves very slowly. A ride takes about half an hour. She can enjoy the view." | **Du:** Sie … , dass es dir schlecht wird, denn … . Eine … . Du kannst die … . |
| *(Oma: Das klingt aber fantastisch.)*<br><br>**Du:** Grandma thinks it … . | "You should hurry. It's London's greatest attraction and you will have to queue (up)." | **Du:** Sie sagt, wir … . Es ist Londons … und wir … . |
| **Du:** Vielen Dank für Ihre Hilfe. | "You're welcome." | **Du:** Sie sagt, dass sie uns … . |

*Rezeption, Empfangsbereich = reception, Empfangschef, -dame = receptionist, Reiseführer = tourist guide,*
*eine Fahrt = a ride, buchen = (to) book, schlecht werden = (to) be / get / feel sick*


ISBN: 978-3-12-581180-5

## Situation 2: Partner B

### At the hotel reception

You are a *thirty-year-old woman* who works as a *receptionist* at a *London hotel*. At lunchtime two German tourists appear at the hotel reception and ask you for some information. Soon you notice that one of them – an old lady – does not speak any English.

| **Listen to your guest and correct his / her mistakes.** | **You, to your guests (in English, of course!)** | **Listen to your guest's interpreting and correct his / her mistakes.** |
|---|---|---|
| "Good morning. Can / May I ask you some questions, please?" | **Du:** Ja, natürlich. Was für ein Problem haben Sie? | „Sie fragt, was unser Problem ist." |
| "We would like to go on a sightseeing tour tomorrow. Would you go by bus or by underground / tube?" | **Du:** Mit dem Bus. Es gibt spezielle Besichtigungsbusse. Ich kann ein Busunternehmen anrufen und zwei Plätze für Sie buchen. | „Sie würde den Bus nehmen. Es gibt spezielle Besichtigungsbusse. Sie kann ein Busunternehmen anrufen und zwei Plätze für uns buchen." |
| "Are there (any) sightseeing tours with German-speaking tourist guides?" | **Du:** Selbstverständlich. Nicht alle deutschen Touristen sprechen perfekt Englisch. | „Selbstverständlich, denn nicht alle deutschen Touristen sprechen perfekt Englisch." |
| "OK, please book a ride / sight-seeing tour for tomorrow morning. She also asks what we can do this afternoon." | **Du:** Oh, das Wetter ist toll. Warum besichtigen Sie nicht das „London Eye"? Es ist nicht weit von hier. | „Sie meint, dass das Wetter toll ist und fragt, warum wir nicht das „London Eye" besichtigen. Es ist nicht weit von hier." |
| "That's a good idea, but I'm sure that Grandma will be / get / feel sick if we go on it." | **Du:** Ich glaube nicht, weil sich das „London Eye" sehr langsam bewegt. Eine Fahrt dauert ungefähr eine halbe Stunde. Sie kann die Aussicht genießen. | „Sie glaubt nicht, dass es dir schlecht wird, denn das „London Eye" bewegt sich sehr langsam. Eine Fahrt dauert ungefähr eine halbe Stunde. Du kannst die Aussicht genießen." |
| "Grandma thinks it sounds fantastic." | **Du:** Sie sollten sich beeilen. Es ist Londons größte Attraktion und Sie werden sich anstellen müssen. | „Sie sagt, wir sollen uns beeilen. Es ist Londons größte Attraktion und wir werden uns anstellen müssen." |
| "Thank you very much for your help." | **Du:** Bitte sehr. / Gern geschehen. | „Sie sagt, dass sie uns gerne geholfen hat." |

*Rezeption, Empfangsbereich = reception, Empfangschef, -dame = receptionist, Unternehmen = company, zwei Plätze = two seats, buchen = (to) book, eine Fahrt = a ride, Aussicht = view, sich anstellen = (to) queue (up)*


Grammar Tandem Activities
ISBN: 978-3-12-581180-5

## Situation 3: Partner A

### Giving directions

You are visiting your *eleven-year-old cousin Fabian* in a *village near Freiburg*. In front of the supermarket a young English couple on a cycling tour through Germany asks you for help because they have lost their way. Your cousin's English is too poor but he knows a lot about Freiburg and the area around. *So he can give you the information and you can do the interpreting*.

| **You, also for your cousin (in English, of course!)** | **Listen to the young Englishman. Correct his mistakes.** | **You, to your cousin (in German, of course!)** |
|---|---|---|
| | "Hello. Are you from here and do you speak English?" | **Du:** Er fragt, ob … und … . |
| **Du:** Mein Cousin wohnt hier, und ich hoffe mein Englisch ist gut genug, um Sie zu verstehen. | "I'm sure. We're on our way to Freiburg. Is there a cycle path near here?" | **Du:** Er sagt, dass sie auf … und will wissen, ob … . |
| *(Fabian: Sie müssen geradeaus fahren bis zur Kirche, dort links abbiegen und die Brücke überqueren. Der Fahrradweg führt (to go) am Fluss entlang.)*<br>**Du:** He says (that) … . | "And how long does it take to get to Freiburg?" / "How much time do we need to get to Freiburg?" | **Du:** Er will wissen, wie … . |
| *(Fabian: Es sind etwa 25 Kilometer. Mit ihrem Gepäck werden sie zwei Stunden brauchen.)*<br>**Du:** He thinks … . | "Everybody says Freiburg is a wonderful city. What can tourists do there?" | **Du:** Er meint … und fragt, was … . |
| *(Fabian: Der Platz um die Kathedrale herum ist berühmt. Man kann das Theater, Kinos oder Museen besuchen und es gibt viele Kneipen und Discos für junge Leute.)*<br>**Du:** My cousin says … . | "Does Freiburg have a youth hostel?" | **Du:** Er will wissen, ob … . |
| *(Fabian: Keine Ahnung – aber es gibt eine Touristeninformation im Stadtzentrum.)*<br>**Du:** He has no …, but … . | "Thank you very much for your tips and, by the way, your English is almost perfect. Goodbye / Bye." | **Du:** Er bedankt … und sagt, dass … . |

*ein Paar = a couple, geradeaus = straight on, Fahrradweg = cycle path, Gepäck = luggage, Platz = square, Kathedrale = cathedral, Kneipe = pub, Touristeninformation = tourist office*

Grammar Tandem Activities
ISBN: 978-3-12-581180-5

# Situation 3: Partner B

## Giving directions

You are a *young English man* on a cycling tour through Germany with your girlfriend. You want to visit Freiburg, but unfortunately you have lost your way. In front of a supermarket in a village you meet two German students and ask them for help. You are lucky – one of them speaks English.

| Listen to the German boy / girl and correct his / her mistakes. | You, to the German boy / girl (in English, of course!) | Listen to the boy's / girl's interpreting and correct his / her mistakes. |
|---|---|---|
| | **Du:** Hallo. Seid ihr von hier und sprecht ihr English? | „Er fragt, ob wir von hier sind und ob wir English sprechen." |
| "My cousin lives here and I hope my English is good enough to understand you." | **Du:** Ich bin mir sicher. Wir sind auf dem Weg nach Freiburg. Gibt es in der Nähe einen Fahrradweg? | „Er sagt, dass sie auf dem Weg nach Freiburg sind und will wissen, ob es in der Nähe einen Fahrradweg gibt." |
| "He says (that) you must ride / cycle straight on to the church, turn left there and cross the bridge. The cycle path goes along the river." | **Du:** Und wie lange dauert es, um nach Freiburg zu kommen? | „Er will wissen, wie lange es dauert / wie viel Zeit sie brauchen, um nach Freiburg zu kommen." |
| "He thinks it's about 25 kilometres. With (all) your luggage you will need two hours." | **Du:** Jeder sagt, Freiburg ist eine wunderbare Stadt. Was können Touristen dort unternehmen? | „Er meint, (dass) jeder sagt, Freiburg sei eine wunderbare Stadt und fragt, was Touristen dort unternehmen können." |
| "My cousin says (that) the square around the cathedral is famous. You can go to the theatre, cinemas or museums and there are a lot of pubs and discos for young people." | **Du:** Hat Freiburg eine Jugendherberge? | „Er will wissen, ob Freiburg eine Jugendherberge hat." |
| "He has no idea, but there is a tourist office in the city centre." | **Du:** Vielen Dank für eure Tipps und übrigens, dein Englisch ist beinahe perfekt. Auf Wiedersehen. | „Er bedankt sich für unsere Tipps und sagt, dass mein Englisch fast perfekt ist." |

*unglücklicherweise = unfortunately, Fahrradweg = cycle path, dauern = to take, Jugendherberge = youth hostel, übrigens = by the way*


Grammar Tandem Activities
ISBN: 978-3-12-581180-5

## Situation 4: Partner A

### On an exchange in a German family

Your English exchange student *Alan, from Dover* has just arrived at your parents' house. But he is very shy and excited, so you decide to speak English today. *You have to do the interpreting* because you are the only English-speaking person in your family.

| **You, also for your parents (in English, of course!)** | **Listen to your English exchange partner. Correct his mistakes.** | **You, to your parents (in German, of course!)** |
|---|---|---|
| *(Mutter: Alan sieht müde aus. Frag ihn, wie seine Reise war.)*<br><br>**Du:** Mum says … . How … ? | "I had a good journey, but it took more than 20 hours and I couldn't sleep on the bus. Now I'm quite / pretty tired." | **Du:** Er sagt, dass … aber … und er … . Jetzt … . |
| *(Mutter: Frag ihn, ob er Hunger hat. Ich habe etwas Leckeres gekocht!)*<br><br>**Du:** Are … ? Mum … ! | "No, thank you. On the journey I ate a lot of sandwiches and sweets. – By the way, your German lemonade tastes very good." | **Du:** Er hat … . Auf der Reise … und … . Unsere … . |
| **Du:** Hättest du gerne noch eine Flasche? | "Yes, please. I'm still thirsty." | **Du:** Er sagt, dass … . |
| *(Vater: Frag ihn mal, ob er sich auf seinen Aufenthalt freut.)*<br><br>**Du:** Dad asks if … . | "Yes, I am. I already feel at home. I think (that) it will be fun to learn German here." | **Du:** Er sagt, dass … und denkt, … . |
| *(Vater: Und deshalb werden wir morgen Deutsch miteinander reden.)*<br><br>**Du:** And that's … . | "I agree. – But now I'm terribly tired. Do you mind if I go to bed now?" | **Du:** Er ist … . Aber jetzt … und fragt, ob … . |
| *(Mutter: Natürlich nicht. Wir wünschen ihm eine gute Nacht, … und sag ihm, dass er morgen ein gutes deutsches Frühstück bekommen wird.)*<br><br>**Du:** Of course not. We … . | "Good night – and thank you very much." | **Du:** Er wünscht … und … . |

*etwas Leckeres = something delicious, sich freuen auf = (to) look forward to, ein Aufenthalt = a stay, deshalb = that's why,*
*wünschen = (to) wish*

Grammar Tandem Activities
ISBN: 978-3-12-581180-5

## Situation 4: Partner B

### On an exchange in a German family

You are *Alan, a fifteen-year-old exchange student from Dover* who has just arrived at his host family's house in Germany. But as you are too shy and excited to say anything in German, your hosts offer to speak English to you today. Your exchange partner does the interpreting.

| **Listen to your German exchange partner and correct his / her mistakes.** | **You, to your German host family – in English.** | **Listen to your exchange partner's interpreting and correct his / her mistakes.** |
|---|---|---|
| "Mum says (that) you look tired. How was your journey?" | **Du:** Ich hatte eine gute Reise, aber sie dauerte mehr als 20 Stunden und ich konnte im Bus nicht schlafen. Jetzt bin ich ziemlich müde. | „Er sagt, dass er eine gute Reise hatte, aber sie dauerte mehr als 20 Stunden und er konnte im Bus nicht schlafen. Jetzt ist er ziemlich müde." |
| "Are you hungry? Mum has cooked something delicious." | **Du:** Nein danke. Auf der Reise aß ich viele belegte Brote und Süßigkeiten. – Übrigens, eure deutsche Limonade schmeckt sehr gut. | „Er hat keinen Hunger. Auf der Reise hat er viele belegte Brote und Süßigkeiten gegessen. Unsere deutsche Limonade schmeckt ihm übrigens sehr gut." |
| "Would you like another bottle?" | **Du:** Ja, bitte. Ich habe immer noch Durst. | „Er sagt, dass er immer noch Durst hat." |
| "Dad asks if you are looking forward to your stay." | **Du:** Ja. Ich fühle mich bereits (wie) zu Hause. Ich denke, dass es Spaß machen wird, hier Deutsch zu lernen. | „Er sagt, dass er sich bereits (wie) zu Hause fühlt und denkt, dass es Spaß machen wird, hier Deutsch zu lernen." |
| "And that's why we will speak German to each other tomorrow." | **Du:** Ich bin einverstanden. – Aber jetzt bin ich schrecklich müde. Habt ihr etwas dagegen, wenn ich jetzt ins Bett gehe? | „Er ist einverstanden. Aber jetzt ist er schrecklich müde und fragt, ob wir etwas dagegen haben, wenn er jetzt ins Bett geht." |
| "Of course not. We wish you a good night, and tomorrow you will get a good German breakfast." | **Du:** Gute Nacht – und vielen Dank. | „Er wünscht uns eine gute Nacht und bedankt sich." |

*dauern* = (to) take, *übrigens* = by the way, *schmecken* = (to) taste, *Haben Sie etwas dagegen, wenn … ?* = Do you mind if … ?


Grammar Tandem Activities
ISBN: 978-3-12-581180-5

# Anhang

## Aufkleber für Hängemappen

1 Comparison of adjectives

2a Conditional sentences (type 1+2)

2b Conditional sentences (type 1–3)

3 Relative clauses

4 Asking questions

5a The passive — or

5b The passive

5c The passive

6a Reported speech

6b Reported speech

6c Reported speech

7 Grammar mix (Amateurs)

7 Grammar mix (Professionals) — 2x3

8 Mediation: Situation …

Grammar Tandem Activities
ISBN: 978-3-12-581180-5